Apartment Property Management

Strategies in Excellence

By

Robert Current

Web-Site: http://www.aptresults.com

E-Mail: bob@aptresults.com

First Edition

Apartment Property Management
Strategies in Excellence

By Robert Current

Published By: Lulu Press Inc

ISBN 1-4116-1019-9

Warning – Disclaimer

This book is designed to provide information in regard to the subject matter covered and is sold with the understanding that the publisher and author are not engaged in rendering legal, accounting or other professional services. If legal or other expert assistance is required, the services of a competent professional should be sought.

Every effort has been made to make this manual as complete and as accurate as possible. However there may be mistakes both typographical and in content. Therefore, this text should be used only as a general guide and not as the ultimate source of information. Further, this book contains information on property management only up to the printing date.

The purpose of this book is to educate and entertain. The author and publisher shall have neither liability nor responsibility to any person or entity with respect to any loss or damage caused, or alleged to be caused, directly or indirectly by the information contained in this book.

If you do not wish to be bound by the above, you may return this book to the publisher for a full refund.

Apartment Property Management
Strategies In Excellence

Introduction 7

Chapter One: The Passionate Manager 15

Chapter Two: Cherish Your Vendors 29

Chapter Three: Learn To Deal With Difficult 37
                    People and Situations

Chapter Four: Resident Retention That Works . . . 53

Chapter Five: Motivate Your Staff To Excellence . . 73

Chapter Six: Leasing Made Simple 97

Chapter Seven: Make It Fun 115

Chapter Eight: Know What They Think 129

Chapter Nine: Use Technology 141

Chapter Ten: Trends To Keep An Eye On 151

Conclusion 168

"There is nothing more difficult to take in hand, more perilous to conduct, or more uncertain in its success, than to take the lead in the introduction of a new order of things, because the innovator has for enemies all those who have done well under the old conditions and lukewarm defenders in those who may do well under the new."

Written by Machiavelli
In The Prince

Introduction

It was more than 28 years ago that I rented my first apartment. Times were certainly simpler back then. I put an ad in the local newspaper and chose the person that I thought would be most likely to pay the rent. No credit check, no employment verification and certainly no criminal background check. The lease was a single page long.

No one in his or her right mind would try or really want to rent in that manner any more. Today everything must be checked and double-checked. Reams of paperwork must be completed and specific procedures carefully followed.

Property management remains one of the few fields where experience is as important as a college degree. You just can't teach someone without people skills how to be a good apartment manager. You can show them how to complete the bookwork but a really good property manager is much more than just an accountant.

The successful manager must also be adept at juggling the needs of the property owners with the reality of the market place. The buck always stops at the managers' desk for anything that happens on the property. You are the one responsible for motivating and directing your staff.

Yet managing an apartment community can also be an extremely rewarding job for someone who can bring passion into their work. Who else provides so many people with their homes? Who else works so hard to make sure that these homes are safe, clean, well heated and cooled? Property managers make sure that the sidewalks are shoveled clear of snow in the winter and the lawns are green and neatly mowed in the summer.

They make sure that the flowerbeds are full of pretty colors in the spring and the parking areas always kept clean and neat. They insure that the pool is squeaky clean and ready to use and the laundry machines well maintained and operating properly.

Anytime a sink faucet leaks or a toilet plugs up they are there to have it fixed for their residents. They are on their property to do this and much more.

While one of the primary tasks of the property manager is to provide homes for their customers they must accomplish this within the budget restrictions provided by the property owners. Every decision must be weighed carefully against maintaining that balance of expenses and income. The successful manager always remembers that it is someone else's money that they are spending.

By default the manager also represents the interests of the owner on property. They must always strive to represent their policies to the staff and residents in the best light.

Today though accomplishing these tasks is a whole lot more complicated than ever before. The current legal climate has helped transform this profession into a quagmire with ever increasing dangers.

Managers must keep abreast with the latest requirements of lead paint, asbestos and fair housing laws. They must be very adept at dealing with clients that can often be angry or upset. Add to that the ever-changing client demands and market conditions that the typical manager must face and you have ample reasons for the burnout that is epidemic in our industry.

Every day as a property manager can contain a new lesson in frustration. Caught between the needs of the typical property owners that you work for and the demands of the residents something needs to give and many times it is the managers peace of mind.

This is why on-site property management staff typically has a huge turnover every year. The constant tension and never ending demands have turned property management into a high stress profession.

Here we are in the 21st century and most of us are still trying to figure out how we can bring some passion and joy into our lives. In a recent survey 49% of Americans stated that they were unhappy with their jobs. This compared to 45% in a 1995 survey.

Every year there are more than thirteen billion doses of tranquilizers, barbiturates, and amphetamines prescribed to help people handle the stress and depression in their lives. Nearly eight million Americans suffer from stress induced stomach ulcers and according to the *International Headache Society* the most common cause for migraines is stress.

And there is a lot of stress in property management work. In fact property management would make an excellent case study in how to create stress in the work place. Not only do on-site managers have the responsibility of running multi-million dollar properties and diverse staffs, they also must deal with people supplying one of their most primal and basic needs – that of shelter.

More than ever property managers need help in dealing with their profession and its challenges. In order to be a successful property manager you must focus on your strengths and develop core policies that will help you and your staff accomplish your jobs. Successfully run properties are those that are:

Customer Driven

Cost Effective

Fast and Flexible

Constantly Improving

This book is a quick and easy guide to identifying some of the policies that will make accomplishing these goals a little easier. Inside are proven strategies that will allow you to make your property more profitable while making your job less stressful and a lot more fun.

Each of the following chapters will introduce a separate strategy that will allow you to do your job faster and more smoothly. A manager must always be adept and creative to accomplish the goals set by the owners using the limited available resources. The goal is to create an environment where a large asset can be managed to its' best advantage. The results of how well this job is done are easily viewed every month in the financial statements.

To accomplish this the typical manager employs a wide range of skills. Financials must be prepared and evaluated, employees must be supervised and motivated, empty apartments must be rented, advertising must be planned, employees trained and unhappy residents calmed and satisfied.

All this makes managing a property an extremely challenging job. Managers are like everyone else in that each has his or her own strengths and weaknesses. The job can be much easier if you recognize what these are and build a team that compliments them.

Meanwhile, each management company also has its own style and goal of management. They each have their own priorities and ways that they want to manage their business.

This can vary depending upon the type of property management they are involved with. There are asset management types that own the properties they manage. There are fee management types that manage properties for a fee. There are large and small companies. Every thing from single-family homes to large apartment communities with hundreds of units must be successfully operated. Each brings its own special needs and knowledge to the table.

For a manager to be successful it is important to understand and accomplish the goals that the owner desires. To bring passion into your work you must also try to do so in a way that will allow you to work with pride.

Most apartment managers typically work between 40 and 60 hours each week. It will vary with the time of the month, the size of the property and the overall workload. That means that somewhere between 40% and 50% of a property managers' available time awake each week is spent at work. With that much time involved in one activity it is important to enjoy what is being done. Why be miserable for half your waking time for the 40 or 50 years of your life that you will work?

National employment estimates show that employment of property managers for all types of real estate are anticipated to increase faster than any other occupation until at least the year 2010.

Many more of these jobs will open as a result of the burnout that occurs daily in this industry. Many positions will open as people leave to seek new jobs in other areas. Bringing passion to your work will allow you to enjoy the benefits while better handling the stress of a career in property management.

This book will introduce concepts that demonstrate how you can accomplish more work in less time. It will show you how to motivate your staff to produce exceptional work.

It will show you how to increase results from the same amount of work by focusing your efforts in the areas that will benefit the most. Most of all it will show you how to relax and enjoy your career in property management.

"The quality of a person's life is in direct proportion to his commitment to excellence, regardless of his chosen field of endeavor."

-- Vince Lombardi--

Chapter One
The Passionate Manager

"Only the best, most passionate people will win this game."

In a perfect world we would all have a job that we loved and in which we had pride. Supervisors would adore us and we would be paid what we felt we were really worth. Well, welcome to the real world. It is hard enough to find just one of these at the typical job let alone all of them.

In order to succeed as a property manager it is important that you take control and transform your job into one where you can prosper and enjoy the work.

The current changing market is forcing employers to examine expenses from top to bottom. Unfortunately many companies seem to be responding by piling an ever-increasing workload on their employees for the same pay scale as a cost cutting measure. This often backlashes as skilled management staff increasingly reach burnout and leave the industry.

The entire business climate that we work in is experiencing a huge shift. The basic ways that companies do business are changing.

The next decade will experience far-reaching shifts in how companies interact with both each other and their customers. Customers will become much more demanding and discriminating. Companies that succeed will do so partly by creating new types of alliances and marketing agreements that will cross industry lines.

To prosper in this brave new world property managers must learn to remain both flexible and creative. Doing things because that is the way they have always been done will be a sure path to failure. The successful manager will be the one that is willing to continually re-examine the core beliefs about how best to do their job. The fact that is both scary and exciting is that the future will continue to bring even bigger changes at an ever-faster pace.

In order to prosper during these changes employees must learn to adapt and be quick on their feet. By constantly training and improving themselves employees can insure that they will not only survive but also prosper. In order to accomplish this we must strive to be the best employee that we can. We need to do this for our employer but even more for ourselves.

To become that best employee we must first make sure that we have a fair and honest understanding of our skills and what it is that comprises our job duties. Only with a candid assessment and evaluation can we hope to set realistic goals for ourselves.

Whether those goals are to stay safe and secure in a current position or to advance in responsibility and compensation, you need to know both where you are now and where you want to go in the future.

Too often we as employees allow ourselves to be lulled into a perception that we are irreplaceable and unable to make mistakes. Anyone who disagrees with us must be wrong or just plain stupid.

Yet this is rarely the complete truth. We misunderstand the situation or the goal that is being pursued by our employer. We need to make sure that we set aside any preconceptions we carry if we hope to see the bigger picture and make sure it is a place where we can prosper.

By honestly examining your strengths and weaknesses you can see which skill areas need to be improved. You can make yourself a more valuable employee by knowing your weaknesses and focus on strengthening those areas or you can even seek another job where they won't matter.

Knowing your weaknesses will also allow you to look for a support staff that will compliment your skills. The choice is always yours and whatever you decide to do having some control will make you happier.

There are actually two basic areas that must be examined to clearly understand your current situation. The first is your actual job skills while the second is your presentation of those skills.

Your presentation is basically how well you position yourself for others to recognize your skills. Survey after survey has shown that how you dress, communicate and act affects how people will perceive you.

Whether we like it or not many lasting impressions are made in the first few seconds of contact every time you meet someone. This includes both your employer and your customers.

Things that are assessed would include your demeanor, dress and hygiene. In order to be successful you must present yourself as someone who already is successful and capable. Many good books have been written on this subject so what follows will be just a quick overview of some basic ideas.

When your potential customers come into your office they will want to find someone who is both professional and honest. They will want someone who is there to help and understand what they want. They will want someone that they can be comfortable with.

Meanwhile your employer is looking for someone they can trust. Someone who will represent them to the public and be able to carry out the assigned duties they need completed.

One time I referred someone from a prior company for a position with the company I was working for at the time. Carol had successfully run the same size property that she was interviewing for. She knew how to run a property and had a lot of experience. Yet when she showed up for the interview she wore a t-shirt and jeans. While this might have been OK if she was going to clean out the pool it definitely was not a good way to make a good first impression. Needless to say, she was not offered the job.

Make sure that you dress professionally at all times. Dress like the person in the position you want if you are interviewing for a new job. Everyone automatically judges the people they meet by how they dress. It may not be fair but that's how it works.

Dressing professionally does not mean you have to wear a suit and tie or its equivalent. Dressing professionally means that you wear the clothes that are appropriate for the position and work. Don't overdress or you can just as easily create the wrong impression for your customers or future employer.

The clothes that you wear must be conservative, clean and fit well. Nothing looks worse than someone who is trying to fit into a size that is too small. Make sure that the length of the sleeves, dresses and trousers are correct. Avoid fad clothes that are more appropriate for personal time.

A seamstress can easily make sure your clothes fit correctly for just a few dollars. Avoid large amounts of jewelry, make-up, aftershave or perfume. Keep your hair neatly trimmed and clean. Facial hair should be conservative and neatly trimmed.

Women should dress especially carefully to create the impression they desire. Don't wear dresses that are too short unless you are applying for a job as a cocktail waitress. Nails should be kept short and neatly trimmed.

Many management companies are still designing their personnel systems to compensate for less skilled employees. In other words they try to centralize decisions to lower the responsibility of the on-site persons to simple bookkeeping and leasing.

However, by designing systems with this in mind and hiring lower skilled people they are ultimately creating more problems than they are solving. Yet they do this because of the limited number of really skilled professionals that are available.

Creating and presenting a professional appearance will give you a leg up on any job interview.

Another current hot trend among many progressive companies is to attempt to flatten the typical company hierarchy. The costs in both time and money to pass decisions up and down a chain of command are no longer feasible. These companies are actively looking for ways to push the decisions down as close to the customer as possible. In order to accomplish this they must find and recruit qualified professionals.

Nowhere will this trend have more impact than in our industry. Everyone has a wealth of knowledge and experiences that they will bring to their jobs if they are allowed that opportunity. Finding the right person for the job and then empowering them to succeed is an extremely strong strategy for running a successful property.

The only thing that we can know for sure is that there will be changes. The way that business is done in this country will continue to change at an ever-increasing pace. Whatever the style your management company uses one of the best defenses that you can utilize to succeed is improving your skills and education. You need to look at yourself as your own best investment.

Without a doubt the best initial opportunities for apartment managers will continue to go to those with college degrees in business administration. However, people with degrees in closely related fields and those with actual experience would also find an open field for success.

Since you can take college courses on-line and most apartment associations offer ongoing classes in a variety of subjects there is no excuse not to improve yourself. You goal should be to make sure that you know more about every aspect of the apartment management business than anyone else in your company.

Don't stop at understanding just the on-site business. Make sure you are a well-rounded big picture kind of person. You need to be able to understand financials and the effect that every day trends will have on them.

Pay attention to new local and national laws and make sure that you understand how they could affect how you conduct business. Keep an eye on trends in other service businesses and try to learn how these new ideas could be used in our industry.

All this won't make you irreplaceable but at least you will become the person hardest to loose. In case of a parting of the ways it will also make sure that you land on your feet and find a new job quickly.

In general, on-site managers are by nature an independent lot. To manage an apartment property you need to be able to be a self-starter with nerves of steel. You need to have rock-solid honesty and an ability to accept large amounts of responsibility without flinching.

In order for you to remain sane you must also be able to enjoy the job. Having fun and doing an exceptionally good job is something that many people will tell you is mutually exclusive. That is just not true.

It is also one of the reasons that turnover will continue to remain so high in property management. Day after day of the normal grind can wear down even the strongest most positive personality. Having fun is so important that there is a separate chapter dealing with having fun at work.

At the same time, if you expect your employees to give you their best work and support you must show them how it is done. You must be their example. Make sure that you are doing your work at the level you expect of your staff. The best way to teach the people you work with to bring excellence and passion into their work is to show them.

You can do this by continually working hard to keep both an open and flexible mind. Go to as many classes and seminars to learn new ideas as you can. Try to attend on as many diverse subjects as possible. Read widely and always keep that open mind.

Even if you disagree with a new idea when it is presented make sure that you examine it from all points both pro and con before dismissing it. Sometimes you will pick up new ideas from the most amazing and unexpected places or people.

When you disagree with somebody, if you understand why you disagree you can better comprehend and explain your position to others. Often disagreeing will cause you to rethink some part of your belief or see it with a slightly different perspective.

As it says in The Art Of War "know your enemy". Everybody has an opinion and all were based on some basic idea or philosophy that made sense at the time and place they were formed.

Just because you might not agree with it doesn't mean that you can't learn something from a conflicting opinion. Always be willing and open to listening to new ideas. Even if you dismiss them as soon as you walk out of the room they still deserve to be heard and many times can teach you a lot.

In order to be at your best you need to achieve and maintain a good and positive attitude. Since as manager you are the on-site representative for the owner you can expect for anyone who has a problem to blame you. Occasionally people will be confrontational and angry. A positive attitude will allow you to keep a cool head and use your people skills to cut through the bull and find a solution.

Going a long ways towards helping you handle any type of situation will be an ability to emphasize and understand what is happening. Remember that when you are dealing with residents the issues involve their homes. Even if you are unable to do anything to help in a given situation the very least you should offer is making sure that you listen.

Taking classes that will improve your people skills will help immeasurably. So don't stop at taking classes that are directly associated with property management. To be successful the typical manager must be one part financial wizard, one part disciplinarian, one part bookkeeper and one part father or mother figure.

The wider the experience and knowledge that you have the better your ability to focus on the big picture will become. You need to be able to step away from the daily problems that scream to be heard and maintain a dispassionate attitude to effectively manage a property.

Focusing only on the small loud problems will cause you to drift into crisis style management. While sometimes situations force this on us it will always take your time away from the more important big picture items that you must accomplish.

Take financial classes. It is important to know and be able to explain what effect different expenses and income have on the bottom line. Understanding how a financial balance sheet works will make it a lot easier to find mistakes that can happen. It will not only allow you to understand exactly how your job affects the bottom line, it will help you explain this to others.

Spend some time taking classes in computers. There are always inexpensive classes available every time a new operating system comes out. When updates of your current word processing or databases happen you should go to classes to learn the latest capabilities. Knowing how to maximize what a program will do for you will make your job that much easier.

Learn to use either a computer PIM (personal information manager) or a day timer to schedule your work each day. In order to maximize your time you must keep organized.

Using a program on your computer to do this will make it easy to schedule and change priorities on the fly. Just as important is that it will allow your staff to know what is going on. It will also encourage your staff to get better at organizing their days. Huge amounts of time are wasted daily in the average office because the work is not planned out.

Keeping your day organized will allow you to handle the things that are thrown at you daily without falling into a crisis mode.

It will also allow you to keep an eye on the big picture items that are important without getting lost in the day-to-day madhouse.

Big projects need to be broken into smaller bites that can be finished each day. If you don't they can seem overwhelming. Learning to do this for yourself will allow you to teach your staff the same idea.

Finally it is extremely important to control how your staff is assigned to you. Everyone has a different management style. Some people will work better with some styles than others.

In order to become the best that you can you must have people around you with which you can work. As manager you need to make sure that every person brought onto your property is interviewed and approved by you. Failure to do this will only complicate your job.

By personally choosing your staff you will be able to choose only the people that have or can develop the mind set to deliver excellence in service. You will be able to choose the support staff that will compliment your strengths and shore up your weaknesses.

Many management companies that still operate in the hierarchical mode will want to control staffing. They do this by controlling who goes where and when. They try to maintain a higher degree of control over the individual properties by controlling the staff.

Many companies of this type also want to discourage the strong team bond that can develop in a well-managed property. They want their employees to have a stronger bond to the management company than to the individual manager or property.

This is both short sighted and counter productive. In order to have the most success on a property a strong team must be formed. The manager must be the head of that team.

Each team member must feel a part of that group and learn to rely upon and help each other. A cohesive team will deliver quality and excellence in ways that are greater as a whole than the individual parts.

You can tell a great team within a few minutes of stepping on a property. The staff is smiling and laughing with each other and their customers. The maintenance radios will be used heavily as each team member supports or looks for help from their co-workers.

Everyone will know what needs to be done each day and his or her part of making sure it does get done on time and correctly. They all see the bigger picture and their part in making it work.

This is the type of team that you will need to create to make your job as easy and enjoyable as possible. That is why you need to control your staffing. When you make the lives of your team easier and more rewarding they will do the same for you.

Encourage your staff to improve their skills just as you are. Helping your staff be successful is a huge step towards your own success. You simply can't do the one without doing the other.

"You'll always have everything in life that you want if you help enough people get what they want."

--Zig Ziglar--

Chapter Two
Cherish Your Vendors

"Make your vendors successful and they will return the favor."

Having good vendors can make your life so much easier that it is worth the extra effort. Much of the work on any property is contracted out to our vendors. Whether it is carpet installation, painting or lawn maintenance we will generally rely on these independent businesses.

Many of the companies that we use specialize in servicing only apartment communities. These companies can be your best friend or a source of your worst nightmares. It is extremely important that you work to create a good relationship with your vendors from the very outset.

It doesn't matter whether it is with a completely new vendor or if your have inherited vendors when you start at a new property. The basic steps that will allow you to form an ongoing connection between you and you vendors are the same.

First, it is important to remember that these vendors talk to each other at various properties and meetings. It is not unusual for them to refer potential business to each other or ask for a reference on specific properties or manager. The last thing that you want to happen is gaining a reputation for dealing harshly with vendors.

The good news is that these referrals will also work both ways. If you treat your vendors fairly it will make you a prime customer whose business is much sought after.

It is extremely important to show vendors that you are a first-class customer because it will motivate them to extend to you their best service and pricing. They can also be an excellent source of referrals for new vendors in non-competing fields when a need arises.

Therefore one of the first steps to finding and keeping quality vendors is to make sure that you treat them fairly. You want to find the vendors that will provide good work and or sell materials to you for a fair price. Notice that I said fair price, not the lowest price.

Vendors are in business just like you and they need to make a profit to survive. If you always try to squeeze every last penny out of any pricing structure they give you they will respond by inflating your pricing quotes to compensate. This will make it harder to insure that you are getting the best quotes without multiple bids.

The key to getting a fair price is to make sure that you clearly communicate your needs to your vendors. You both must understand exactly what you are asking for and when. A clearly written request for proposal outlining your exact needs should be a standard part of any larger purchase. If you clearly express your requirements you will be able to get competitive pricing while still allowing the vendor to earn a fair profit.

Any lasting relationship always involves give and take on both sides. Be reasonable in your needs and listen to your vendors' suggestions to create a win for both of you.

Another huge factor a vendor will use to determine their price structure is whether you are going to be a one-time client or if you are looking for a long-term relationship. Never be afraid to blow your own horn about the amount of business that a vendor can expect from you. Just remember to base it on reality. Showing a vendor that establishing a long-term relationship is your goal is always a good way to clearly communicate that you are willing to trade ongoing business for quality, timing and pricing.

This can only happen if both of you make sure that you clearly understand what it is that you each expect from the other.

Good communication should also mean that if you are unhappy about a service or product you must let the vendor know. Problems will always arise so make sure to use them. Any good vendor, one you will want to keep, will be eager to fix any problems that you have.

Make sure that your expectations are reasonable and that you are always willing to listen. A vendor who is successful remains that way by constantly looking for ways to improve their service and find better products.

You don't have time to acquire their experience and knowledge and once you establish a good working relationship you won't need to. First-rate vendors should know what works and what doesn't. They will have much more experience with their product or service than you so it is to your advantage to make sure that you use it.

Another important facet in maintaining a long-term relationship is to make sure that you abide by whatever payment terms you have agreed on. For heaven sakes pay your vendors on time or even better yet pay them early.

It seems that the larger the management company the longer it can take to get a check out of them. Paying on time seems to rank near the bottom of priorities for many management companies while it is always near the top for your vendors.

Nothing is more frustrating for a vendor than an apartment client that ignores agreed payment terms. These payment terms are the lifeblood of the vendors. Without a steady predictable cash flow, these companies cannot budget with any accuracy and are required to maintain large cash reserves or take out loans to pay expenses. One way or another these costs will eventually be passed on to you.

Typically, the excuse that apartment management companies regularly use is that it takes thirty days or longer to process the bills. In a word - bull.

Remember that apartment complexes require that all their residents pay rent in advance. After the due date large late fees and ultimately eviction is the consequence for every late payment. It is important that you play by your own rules when you are paying your vendors. This will result in you receiving both better pricing and faster more reliable service.

Every vendor also structures their pricing and service schedule based to a certain extent on how fast they get paid. A lot of smaller management companies' instinctively seem to know this and use it to their benefit. The faster you pay, the better service and pricing you will receive. Vendors always know who pays and who stalls. The properties that pay on time will always get the best and fastest service.

At the same time it is just good management to have a primary vendor in each area of use along with a backup. Let each vendor know up front that you are doing this to avoid future problems. In case of some emergency where you need a product or service sooner than your primary contractor can deliver you will still have that back up. The back up vendor will just be waiting for that chance to show you how well they can perform.

This will also result in some gentle arm-twisting to remind your primary vendors know that they are in a competitive market and need to keep on their toes. At the same time it will keep you up to date on the going prices for your needs. As long as you are honest and up front with both vendors about why you are doing this they will understand and respect your reasons.

The best part is that if for some reason the primary vendor can't do the job at all any more, you have already proven to the backup vendor that you are a client worth your weight in gold. You have shown them that you will be both an honest and loyal customer.

They will already know what you want and expect and will be able to hit the ground running so you don't miss a step. Just remember that then you need to go out and get a new backup vendor.

There is a trend among larger management companies that I find disturbing. Every year they want their vendors to supply "gifts" to be given away at the company Christmas parties. These companies go to the vendors and demand presents with the implied threat that there will be less business if they don't comply.

Most companies have policy manuals that require their managers to refuse gifts from vendors over a certain amount. This is to keep the managers from feeling obligated to do business with certain vendors. I don't understand why this rule changes once the kickbacks get to the corporate level.

The amounts of gifts that are collected are never that large. Yet as a vendor I know that it feels like an extra gouge each year whether you know it is coming or not. I feel that the management companies should save their integrity and buy their own gifts.

Another disturbing trend is having a master list from the corporate office of "approved vendors". These are usually the vendors that have been beaten down the most in their pricing. Inevitably getting to their lowest price seems to involve trimming corners on the quality.

We need to remember that each property has its own needs and quirks. Just because a vendor works well with one manager or property doesn't mean that the relationship will work as well for another. If anything, my experience is that once a vendor has a master contract they tend to supply poorer service.

The successful relationship between a manager and his or her vendors is one that developes over time. That type of relationship is one that will allow the manager to call and ask for special favors of their contact in case of emergency.

There will also be a comfort level there that won't be when someone is forced down the managers' throat. While it is a good idea to share names of quality vendors in a master vendor list it should be the managers that control which ones are put on it and whom they will ultimately use.

Some cause happiness wherever they go; others, whenever they go.

--Oscar Wilde--
[Playwright]

Chapter Three
Learn To Deal With Difficult People and Situations

"If you can't say something nice about your supervisor it might be time to look for new job."

Learning how to deal with difficult people can be a daunting task. Sometimes it seems that it would be ever so much easier if we just didn't have to deal with other people. There are days that seem like every person coming into your office is demanding something. Often these people will be angry and upset.

Part of the reason is that our high tech high-speed world is causing people more stress than ever before. Often they will come into your office after a long stress filled day of their own and dump on the first person they encounter. Or your supervisor calls you right after coming out of a meeting where his or her boss chewed on them. These people aren't necessarily mean they just are stressed by the world around them.

Unfortunately, then there are the people who are just plain nasty. They don't really care if you are trying to help them or not. They just want their way and don't care how they get it. They will be rude, pushy, obnoxious and malicious to get things their way.

Unfortunately every apartment complex seems to have at least a few of this type of resident. You have my condolences if you have the misfortune of having someone like this for a boss.

Dealing With Difficult Supervisors

Supervisors that make your job infinitely harder and more difficult are unfortunately pretty common. They seem to thrive on making everyone around them miserable. They have little or no loyalty to anyone's needs but their own.   Failure to accomplish any of their goals will bring their wrath upon you. You swear that this type of supervisor stays up late at night thinking of new ways to torment you.

Anyone who has worked for any length of time has had at least one experience with this type of person. They come in all shapes and sizes. They work for big companies and small. I don't know if there is a special training school out there for them but if you ask around everybody seems to know about someone like them.

I had a supervisor like this at one of the properties I managed. It seemed that we disliked each other from the first time we met. I managed to survive for some time until there was one final incident that made me quit and leave a company where I had otherwise enjoyed working.

I had been sent out of town to set up a new property. I was to set up the residents in the computer, organize the files and establish accounts with the vendors that would be needed. During the week that I was away a fellow manager was assigned to look after my property. After a long week of twelve to fourteen hour days I arrived back home late on a Saturday night.

That Monday morning as I was walking the property this supervisor pulled into the parking lot. She was there to do an unscheduled surprise inspection. Even though I had been out of town for the last week she wrote me up for a number of minor problems including trash around the dumpster area.

Then she told me that since I had been written up I would no longer be able to start a new project for the corporate office that I had been excited about. That was the final straw and by that afternoon I had e-mailed my resignation to her.

The funny part is that apparently she even stretched the truth to her supervisors. Imagine my surprise when a few weeks later in a conversation with one of the company owners he expressed disappointment that they were unable to change my mind about leaving.

This same supervisor had apparently told him that she had attempted to talk me out of leaving when she had never even bothered to try. I would be willing to bet that she was dancing on her desk when my resignation came in and never had any intention of allowing me to be talked into staying.

I've also worked for people who I didn't necessarily like but who were total professionals. Even though we often didn't see eye to eye on issues they generally looked at the bottom line and didn't get into petty power trips. They would let you win as long as they also won.

I even remember one supervisor who laid it out for me very plainly. He disagreed with how I managed my staff and property. Yet I always made the budget and all the work was completed on schedule. He told me very honestly that as long as the numbers were OK he would let me run the property as I saw fit. If the numbers ever went south though, I would be fired, period. That created a clear-cut situation that I could deal with and I appreciated his honesty.

One thing that you need to watch for is when a supervisor is dishonest in their dealings. One tactic that these people will use is trying to get you to agree to impossible goals.

If for instance the supervisor I mentioned above wanted to raise the rents above what you thought reasonable she would ask you to just try the new rates for a little while. Once you had agreed to try she would go back to the corporate office and report that you had agreed you could get the higher rates. That way if the new rates failed, she could dump the blame solely on you.

In another case I heard that this same area manager screwed a fellow manager who worked on another property. This talented manager had finally reached the end of her rope and given notice. She had accepted another job and given a two-week notice. The area manager talked her out of the notice by saying how valuable she was and protesting that they didn't want to loose her.

Unfortunately that manager decided to stay and give this company another chance. Just a month later the same area manager fired her when she found someone to replace her at a slightly lower rate of pay. She never even bothered to give the manager any notice.

The bottom line is that you have to look out for yourself because no one else will. While the majority of supervisors are simply looking out for different priorities there are some who would screw their mother to make themselves look even a little better. As long as theirs needs and yours coincide all is well but look out when they don't. These are the people you need to protect yourself from.

If you are already working for someone like that I would suggest you start looking for a new job. This business is hard enough without having to guard your back every minute.

Your relationships with a supervisor are also complicated by the subtle difference in goals that each of you is trying to accomplish. This difference lies in our perception of what it is that our business produces and sells.

Most successful on-site managers realize that they are in the business of selling a service. They realize that apartments are basically just boxes. Each of these boxes will vary in size and amenities but in the end they all serve the same need.

They supply shelter for our residents and any box will put a roof over your head. When an apartment renter needs a new apartment they will first look for the area they want to be in. Then they start shopping for the boxes in that area that are in their price range. They will compare the cost of each box to the benefits they perceive they will receive by renting it.

The interesting thing is that every survey that I have ever seen ranks the attitude and friendliness of the property staff above the amenities when it comes to that final decision. In other words if any two of these boxes are roughly the same in price, location and amenities, the final decision will be based on which staff the prospect likes the best.

Any successful on-site manager that realizes this will strive to make this work for them. They will stress the services that are supplied with their property when they show any prospect their boxes.

Corporate staff on the other hand tends to look at it from a different angle. They see the box as just a box and the people that move in and out of them as just numbers.

So while the on-site staff gets to meet and know the residents the corporate people see just numbers. It could be argued that they are looking at a bigger picture and it is through these numbers that they are being judged.

They are selling themselves to their supervisors and ultimately the owners or their representatives. Therefore they are basically selling a financial product and not a service. Service to them is only what you provide to maintain the investment.

One typical place where this difference can be found is in the handling of work orders. An on-site manager who stresses service would press for at the most a 24 hour turn on work orders. They know that a large part of resident retention is based upon providing superior service. Meanwhile the corporate supervisor would be more inclined to allow two or three days per work order. They are looking more at the costs of providing the service and less at the benefits.

I remember one meeting where a supervisor was actually yelling at me because I refused to allow work orders to sit for two to three days. My mind set was so strongly set on customer service that I refused to comply and was willing to loose my job over that small issue.

It was only later that I started to get a glimmer of why he was so adamant. When I started to understand where our differences came from I started to get a little better at packaging my approach to what he needed while still maintaining my way of servicing my residents.

Remember that the typical management company provides much more than just the service of property management. They are also providing the financial services of managing an investment for the owners and must show a certain level of performance to be successful. This packaging requires that they maintain a different focus at the corporate level.

Yet despite these differences, the bottom line is that we need to work with our supervisors. Part of our job is to give them what they need to accomplish their job.

Over the years the one common complaint that I hear from on-site managers is that the amount of paperwork has increased dramatically. Part of this is because of the legal climate that we live in. It seems that the only way to cover your butt is to have reams of paperwork to prove that everyone has been treated the same. Nobody is trusted unless everything is signed and documented.

This is another example of the difference in what on-site and corporate staff produces. The paperwork is the product that allows corporate to show their investors they report to what they are doing and that they are looking out for their best interests.

Every on-site manager thus gets caught in the middle of that transition from service to product demands.

One day the manager has Miss Jones from unit 108 come into the office because she is upset over a recent rent increase notice and threatens to move-out. The manager knows that Miss Jones is a good resident that has always paid her rent on time, never disturbs her neighbors and has lived in her unit for several years with minimal work orders. That makes her a good resident that we should want to satisfy and keep in her unit.

The corporate supervisor only sees unit #108 as one of a couple hundred where they are trying to build up the average rent per unit and increase the gross income on the property. They need to look more at the property averages than any single resident.

Meanwhile the manager knows that if Miss Jones moves they are going to have to turn the unit and rent it causing them even more work and hassle. Corporate will push from the top while the resident pushes from the bottom and that leaves the manager caught in the middle. This is yet another one of the reasons that the typical property staff has such a huge turnover.

The only way to accomplish both of the above goals is to accept that ultimately you are working for the supervisor and need to supply them with what they need. However, always be looking for ways to streamline and simplify your work. Look for ways to put your personal spin on everything you do.

While the corporate office will always be looking for that paperwork they won't always be looking for ways to allow the manager to do it more simply. The corporate supervisor just needs those numbers.

The bottom line is that this business is constantly changing and evolving. When you find someone that has something to teach you, soak it up. But when you are in a place where someone you report to fills your days with anger and tension it is time to move on.

Problem Residents

Then there are your current residents. There always seem to be a certain limited number of people that cause you the largest percentage of problems.

You may have heard of the 80/20 rule. It states that 80% of your problems are causes by 20% of your residents. Thus 80% of your time spent collecting late rents is caused by 20% or less of your residents. More than 80% of your noise complaints are caused by 20% of your residents.

While the actual percentages will change from property to property the basic theory remains valid. Most of the hastle of your job is caused by a small percentage of your residents. Learning to minimize and control the problems caused by this small group will dramatically affect the complexity of your job.

Collecting the rents is a very important part of managing any apartment complex. Those rents are what pay for the entire operation. Many managers view this as their least favorite part of the job. Taking the hard line that is often needed to collect the rents is not fun nor is it popular.

The basic thing that you must always remember is it is not your money you are collecting. It belongs to the owners of the property. They have invested a lot of capital in their property and the only way that they will continue to do so is if they get a fair return on their investment.

The first step to making sure that collections remain as small a problem as possible is to make sure you qualify your prospects correctly before they move into your apartment. Making sure that they are financially qualified to rent at your property will catch a lot of problems before they even start.

Next, stress the importance of paying the rent on time to each of your new residents. Either you or a member of your staff must explain exactly what will happen if it does not get paid. Explain to everyone that you are required by the owner to take immediate steps if the rent is not received when it is due.

Make sure that your residents understand that communication is the key. If a resident is going to be late let them know that it is in their best interest to communicate with you. The natural inclination of most people is to ignore the problem and hope that they get the rent together before anything bad happens.

Even your best residents will occasionally be late. Don't be embarrassed if you have to post an eviction notice. Then stick to your guns. Charge the late fees as agreed. When the resident communicates with you they are going to be embarrassed and often will try to cover for this by acting angry.

Make sure that you do not respond in the same manner. Let them know that you understand. Let them explain what the problem is to you. It won't make any difference in how you proceed but it will make them feel that you are listening to them.

Make sure that you explain to them that you are simply the owners representative and have very narrowly defined options for handling the situation. Tell them about what will happen and when it will happen in the eviction process. Explain when additional charges will accrue and how much they will be. Ask the resident how they think they are going to be able to catch up and if their next rent is going to be on time.

Not only are there potential fair housing problems if you handle any situation differently but you will be training your residents that there is wiggle room. Allowing this will only cause this same problem to appear again and again.

Occasionally you will run into a situation where that resident just is not going to be able to get caught up. They are either too far behind or just not in a situation where they will be able to catch up fast enough.

Keep a list of agencies both public and private that might help your resident. Stress again that the clock is ticking and you can't stop it. Make sure they know when the clock runs out.

Then follow through. Do not give an inch. On the rent due date make sure that there are timely posting of notices and all notices are followed through on. Keep notes on each notice of any contact that you have with the resident and any dates they give you for when they are going to pay. But the clock never stops.

If you take a fair and consistent stance every time this situation comes up the resident will know what to expect. They will know that you will need to follow policy and won't blame you when it is followed. Knowing this will make them think several times before they shift paying their rent to the bottom of the bill pile.

In contrast to the supervisors and people that are late paying their rent there are always a few troublemakers.

Chronic Complainers

These are the people who just don't get it or care if they are causing other people problems. They are the ones who think that if they yell loud enough or demand nastily enough they will get their way.

Or they might be the ones that just don't understand or care that they are disturbing people when they have parties till late at night or come into the building yelling and hollering.

These people are just plain rude and activities like the ones above must immediately be addressed. Even if you talk to the resident you need to follow up with a notice that explains what they did, what part of the lease it violates, and what is going to happen if they do it again.

Residents that disturb their neighbors' quiet enjoyment of their units are going to end up causing people to move. If you don't immediately stop these disturbances they will only continue and the more that this happens the harder it is to get back under control.

From the day that people move in to the day that they move out, you need to train them in what is acceptable and unacceptable behavior. Loose control of your property and watch the turnover skyrocket. If a resident can't fit into the community by all means let them leave. It is far better to let someone out of their lease early than it is to force them to stay and make the 95% of your residents that are following the rules miserable.

Anytime a good resident moves out you need to check all the units around them. Often times you'll find someone who is disturbing all their neighbors but no one has complained because they thought there was nothing that could be done.

Then there are the really nasty residents. Invariably they will come into your office with stories about how this person or that person is making their life miserable.

Often it will be about a new resident. You need to learn quickly to identify who these people are. Always check the story because many times they can be an early warning of future troubles but you must verify what they say.

There is a lot that you can do if a resident is one of the nasty ones. First rule in dealing with a nasty person is to remain calm. If you get upset you are just playing into their game. That is what they want.

Remember to keep everything in writing. Keep a daily log of your activities in the office. It will help with both residents and supervisors if you can show what was actually happening. If a resident is upset, being nasty, and won't calm down, simply ask them to leave. Tell them to please put their complaint in writing and make sure that it is included in your files.

Anything that they send you should also be kept in their file where it can be easily accessed. Sometimes if a person is in nasty mode they won't stop at you but will try to get you in trouble with your supervisor. Having a clear paper trail will help you show how reasonable you are being.

You should always respond to any letter or complaint that you receive. Once you frame your reply make sure to drop the resident a short note explaining what you can do or not do and include it in your file.

Of course you can always take the step of not renewing at their next lease renewal but that should only be considered as a last step. Keeping your units full is one of your primary objectives and kicking someone out is going in the wrong direction.

If it is someone that you really can't deal with go ahead and get rid of them. If it is someone that you can train though you might want to work with him or her.

A lot of times these people will back off if it is made clear to them that they aren't going to be able to get what they want and what it will cost them if they continue.

Often I have taken the tact of apologizing because I know how unhappy they are. Then I say, in writing, that since they are so unhappy I am willing to allow them to break their lease and move out.

I make it clear that they must abide by the rules for notice and cleaning but otherwise there will be no penalty charges. However, I say that they can move if they are so unhappy.

It is amazing how fast they can get over problems if it starts to become an inconvenience for them.

Creative Complaining

In certain situations complaining may be the right thing to do but make sure that you do it right. When you run into a situation that is frustrating or annoying, complaining gives you an outlet. To make your complaining effective you need to follow a few simple rules.

To begin with don't make it personal. If you attack a person directly they will become defensive. You can complain about an issue or about a problem but if you go beyond this you probably will loose your chance to get a resolution.

Make sure that your complaint is legit. Don't whine about every little thing or you'll be like the boy who cried wolf. Make sure that you have a justifiable complaint and make sure that you choose your battles carefully.

Make sure that you complain to the correct person. Find the one that can actually help you. Don't complain willy-nilly to every person that will listen to you or you'll get a reputation as a whiner.

Finally, make sure that you have an alternative. By having an alternative you will be more likely to get the outcome that you want.

Life is too short to spend your days frustrated and upset. Not only is it unhealthy but also why waste the time. There is always someone out there you can enjoy working with and will appreciate your special skills. You just have to find them.

Finally remember that everyone has the right to his or her own opinion. Everyone is not going to agree with you. Just because someone disagrees with you does not mean that they are wrong. Their need or desire has just as much validity as yours.

Compromise is what makes the world work. What you need to do is sort the reasonable requests from the crazy ones. Work with the first and contain the later.

"Insanity is doing the same thing over and over and expecting a different result."

--Albert Einstein--

Chapter Four
Resident Retention That Works

"If you don't take care of your residents some one else will."

Servicing our residents is the reason that we are in this business. Whether you look at it from an operations or a financial standpoint there would be no need for apartments buildings, managers, supervisors or management companies if not for our residents need for housing.

The process of keeping your residents from moving out of your property and into someplace else is called resident retention. Some estimates place the number of move-outs that could be prevented as high as 65%. This means that as much as 65% of the people that move out of your apartments might be persuaded to stay if the right management approach or strategy was used.

If you listen, residents will always tell you in one way or another what it is that you need to do to make them stay. The trick is learning to listen when they want to talk.

All resident retention activities are by and large based on a combination of both policies and the training given to your staff. It is how well you use these methods that will encourage your residents to stay.

Part of the problem is that most properties generally budget a small amount of money each month for what they call resident retention activities. This allows the typical property to have retention activities that will involve various holiday or activity parties and that is about it. That is because that is all they can afford with the money that they have.

This makes it seem like if you just had the right party or activity the residents would not move out. This is just not true or reasonable. In reality resident retention or lack of it permeates every single aspect of how you do business. Every single contact, whether it is by phone, mail, notices, activity or in person tells your resident how much you want them to stay.

The resident in turn is telling you through their every contact exactly what it is that you need to do to keep them happy and have them stay. You just need to learn how to listen closely.

Sometimes people just have no choice but to move out of your community. Their job is taking them out of the area or their needs change for the type of unit they want. Maybe they are getting married or divorced or having a baby. Other times they just think they have to move. A lot of times if you ask you can discover the core reason they are moving is something that you can help them with.

Part of the problem is that we need to redefine resident retention. The old definition would be keeping your resident in their present apartment. Outside forces are going to change our business from top to bottom. To succeed in this changing marketplace where your customer is ever more demanding and mobile will require a different view.

A better up to date definition of resident retention might be any activity or policy that encourages a long-term business relationship with a resident. This would mean not just at their current apartment but also in other size and style units. It would include not just in your property but also in any other property. It would mean not just while they were living on your property but also even after they moved onto home ownership.

As our resident needs change we need to become more flexible in dealing with them. If a resident wants to move into a larger or smaller unit size doesn't it benefit us to satisfy that need?

Remember how much it costs in advertising just to get someone to come onto our property to look at a unit. Here is someone who already has a beginning of a relationship with us. How much should we be willing to invest in keeping them happy?

Just as important, what if they need a unit style that you don't have available? Many of us work for companies that have multiple properties in their portfolio with different styles of apartments. Yet how much information do we have on our sister properties? How many times a week have you referred someone to another property or had them send someone to you?

Very few if any management companies have a system set up to share information between properties. Every property in a management group should have complete access to the available units and property information on every other property.

The managers and leasing agents should be required to tour each property so they know what they are like and what they offer. We work hard to please our residents. Why do we allow our relationship with them to end just because they need to move to a different area?

Even if there is not a sister property that you can refer the resident, you still need to be careful that the relationship is positive. It is extremely beneficial to maintain files on the properties around you.

If a competitor in the area has what the potential resident needs it can create an extremely positive impression by referring them there. Remember that they are also spending a lot of money on advertising to get people on their property. You can easily create a relationship where referrals go back and forth between you and each of you benefits from residents that might not have otherwise stopped.

It is also unfortunate that many companies act like when a resident leaves it is their last chance to charge as much as they can in fees and misc. charges. Instead we should be focusing on making a good last impression.

Literally hundreds of referrals can come from past residents. If a resident feels that they were treated fairly by a property they will remember that fact for a long time. If they have a family member, friend or co-worker ask them for a referral they will remember you. If they decide to move back into your area you will be the first one that they check on.

At the same time the memory of a bad or ambivalent stay will be remembered just as long. Remember this next time someone is upset about your service. Residents have very long memories and they talk to a lot of other potential residents.

Yet the main focus on most properties continues to be leasing to new residents even as current residents move out. This is equivalent to guarding the front door while leaving the back door wide open. Resident retention is the idea that if you can keep residents from moving you won't need to rent to new people. Every person who stays is one less apartment for which you have to find someone new.

Our industry typically accepts a turnover rate of residents between 90% and 200% per year as normal. This means that we need to rent each apartment an average of once or twice a year just to stay in the same place. Even with the current trend towards a more mobile society this is an extremely expensive number to swallow.

Having a well-run resident retention program in place will allow you to drastically trim that turnover rate. Cutting that rush of residents out your back door can save you in terms of both time and money. Properties that work to retain their residents can achieve a turnover of 90% or less. At an average turnover cost of $1500-$2500 per unit the savings are substantial.

The average turnover cost consists of a variety of different expenses. Everything from the actual rental income that is lost because the apartment is vacant to the costs of advertising and extra maintenance. There are cleaning costs and replacement costs if carpet and vinyl needs updating. Window coverings might need updated, appliances replaced and the unit painted. Maintenance will also need to change locks, re-caulk sinks and tubs and numerous other items. Finally somebody needs to clean up the unit to make it market ready.

All that is before you can even try to rent the unit. Once a unit is ready you must advertise to get people to stop by and look at it. Then there is the time that the leasing staff must spend to show every prospect that comes in what you have. This involves not only the time that is spent showing vacant units to prospects but also the time and cost of all the paper work that must be completed. The advertising must be created and the phones answered to entice prospects to come look at the property.

Applications must be taken and verified and new lease files completed.

Just look at the amount of money that can be saved by successfully using resident retention. Lets assume that you are on a property that has 200 units and a turnover rate of just 120% per year. Make the further assumption that you manage to trim turnover to 90% after aggressively implementing your resident retention program.

This means that your turnover would drop by 30% per year. You would need to turn sixty less apartment units at an average of $2000 per unit. That would save you at least $120,000 per year. That is money that would go directly into your bottom line as profit. Not only that, imagine how much more time you and you staff would have available to service your current residents if you have sixty less apartments to turn and lease every year.

Most apartment properties are run as profit centers. Each property must generate more money than it spends in order to be feasible. Since even an extra 5% in income can make the difference between mediocre and stellar financial performance resident retention is far too valuable a tool to ignore.

Resident retention at its core is both a policy and training issue. It cannot be just throwing a party every once in a while. It is not simply telling your residents to stay. You have to prove to them that you want them to stay and continue to prove it every single day. You must learn to listen to your residents so they can tell you exactly what they need to keep them happy.

When mission statements first started to gain popularity apartment management companies took to them with a vengeance. For years there were lofty goals and statements. For most communities that was where it stopped. Resident retention must be much more hands on and pervasive to succeed.

We are now in the midst of a dynamically changing business climate. What was acceptable five years ago will no longer suffice. Five years from now the differences will be even more profound. Customer expectations and loyalties have become a constantly shifting target. We must remain vigilant and fast on our feet to win our customers business.

An additional complicating factor is that we are seeing a basic shift from a seller to a buyers market in our industry today. Customers want what they want and they want it now. Loyalty is going to have to be constantly earned.

This shift will be covered more extensively in the chapter on future trends but remember that this is going to change how we do business at it's most basic levels.

The changes will come partially because the Internet that is available to us right now is an infant compared to what it will be in coming years. Those changes will cause massive increases in how fast and easily we can handle and use information. Huge amounts of information will be easily retrieved and cross-referenced.

This will make it possible for our customers to access information about our property and the competing properties around us in seconds that would have taken hours or days before. This access to information is going to put increasing power in the customers' hands.

This increased speed will also allow us to make ever more massive amounts of information about our property available on the Internet. Our prospects will have access to pictures, demographic information, crime statistics, surrounding stores in the area, commuting information and property amenities. It will eventually become a standard policy to post the actual units available and their costs.

Customer Satisfaction

It is also just a matter of time until prospects will be able to access information on how well we manage our properties. How hard we work to keep our residents happy.

Think of it this way. What will it be like when every resident that is interested in your property knows exactly how happy or unhappy your current and past residents are with the services you provide? When we live in an era when they can compare your property to the property across the street and see who delivers the best value for their residents.

If that doesn't make you a little nervous you probably both strongly believe in and practice resident retention or you are pretty naive. If you don't believe that this will happen just take a look at Ebay.

This mammoth on-line auction site was founded on the principal of customer service. After each transaction every buyer and seller is asked to rate their experience by how well they were treated. Then these responses are posted in a public area where any one who is thinking about doing business with either party can readily check.

When you think about it this is exactly what we as apartment managers are doing to our residents right now. We research the background of applicants to see if they are someone we want to deal with. The only reason that applicants have been unable to do the same to us is the information has been unavailable.

Once this type of information becomes easily accessed by our prospective residents that is when resident retention will become even more important than it is today. The information will be out for everyone to see whether you are a good landlord or not.

Employee Training

Employee training that teaches the concept of resident retention to your entire staff is an essential first step. Always remember that your maintenance and cleaning staff are the ones that will see your residents most often. Generally the average office staff will see your residents only when leases are signed or if there is some type of a problem.

Your residents will view the attitudes of your staff towards them as reflective of their training and the attitudes of the on-site manager and owners. The manager must work hard to set the proper tone for the property in order for the staff to integrate it into their daily work ethics.

Every staff member must be trained to focus first on servicing the residents. They must be reminded that without residents there would be no need to have a staff in the first place.

A core truth in our changing business is that "no news is not good news". Just because we don't hear from a resident does not mean that they are happy. We need to make sure every contact a resident has with the property staff is used to create a positive impression and foster better communication.

Given an opportunity the resident will tell you what they need to be happy but you have to listen. The entire staff needs to look at every complaint as an opportunity to deliver superior resident service.

It's only when your residents become too annoyed or sure that a complaint is a waste of their time that you begin to loose them.

Even worse is that many of your residents may be a part of the silent majority. They won't complain about things or if they do it will be quietly and infrequently. You need to be listening and watching and your staff must be trained to do the same if you are going to hear the concerns of these residents.

Too many offices also strive for a level of professionalism that is too far above the demographics of the property and residents that they serve. Often when you go into a leasing office you will be greeted by a snobby attitude disguised as professionalism.

This can cause residents to feel uncomfortable when they come into the office. This is the exact opposite of the effect that you should want to create. Be careful what impression you are creating because especially initial impressions are hard to change.

Therefore, every resident that comes into the office must be warmly greeted with a welcoming "how can I help you" attitude. Give them the courtesy of standing and a friendly greeting.

Your staff should be trained to adopt an open body posture to indicate to the resident that you are available to listen and help them. Don't cross your arms and make sure that you face them directly. When you talk to them pay attention and truly listen.

If you are currently helping another resident or prospect, when they come in ask them if they can wait for just a minute. If you are on the phone ask them the same thing. When you talk to them make sure to focus on them and not be distracted by other things happening in the office.

If the phone rings and the conversation with your resident is fairly light ask them if you can answer the phone real quick. Take a message and get back to your resident. Let them know by your actions that they are important and you want to help them. If the conversation is fairly intense or the resident is upset let the phone ring. You can get the message from voice mail later.

If it appears that the resident is there to complain try to sit or stand lower than the resident and don't place a desk between you. If you are taller than the resident you can sit on the edge of a desk or in a chair to lower yourself. Always greet them with a smile whether you know that they are there to complain or not. Invite them to sit down in an area where you can talk privately.

If you are at your desk ask them to sit down and seat yourself. Then encourage the resident to fully explain their problem. Give them your total attention. Don't interrupt until they are finished and then ask any questions you need to be able to fully understand the complete situation.

Many times when a resident comes to you with a complaint they will realize that there is nothing you can do but they just want someone to listen to their frustration.

Make sure that you always ask, "what is it that you want me to do to satisfy you?" You need to know what it is they expect. Most of the time the resident will not have thought the issue all the way through but they will appreciate you asking.

Even if they don't openly show it, having you ask will strike just the right chord for the resolution of whatever problem they are presenting. You have just placed yourself on their side. You have taken the time to listen and tried to find out what they need.

If you can fix the problem do so immediately. Tell the resident exactly what you are going to do, when you are going to do it and then do it. If at all possible while they are still there.

If you can't fix the problem, tell them clearly and fully why not. Explain to them the reason. Also if you can't solve their problem try to offer them some alternatives. Give them something to balance the problem.

If you follow these steps the majority of the time the resident will be thanking you for helping them and apologizing for being angry when they leave.

It is extremely important to remember that a resident's future behavior is often based on their attempt to be consistent with current expectations. In other words, if they are happy with you the resident will look for ways to continue to be happy with you in the future. The same works if they are unhappy. They will look for things to justify how they feel. In either case you need to keep a firm grasp of the big picture when you deal with your residents and work hard to win their loyalty.

Starting A New Relationship

An important consideration to remember is that just like anything else many problems can be created or solved based on how the relationship with the resident is initially started. The first step is to examine the leasing sequence carefully to make sure that an enthusiastic leasing agent isn't over promising your community.

This is also the main reason not to use model apartments. Without fail they are always the units that will show the community in it's best light. They are always facing into landscaping and never next to the parking lots.

If there is a playground or pool it is of in the distance so the noise will be far away. It will usually be a unit that gets good light and will definitely be the most upgraded with the newest appliances, carpet and vinyl.

When a prospect comes in the lights will be on and music playing in the background. The unit will be professionally furnished to maximize the space and make it look its absolute best. Many companies even place leasing applications in the model so they can be filled out on the spot.

The problem is that the prospect is not going to live in the model. They are going to live in the vacant apartment that you have available with their furniture. The carpet and appliances may be older but your prospect isn't going to know that until they move in. The location may be right next to the laundry room and they'll hear banging all evening long. Is it any wonder that we experience turnover like we do? This could almost be classified as bait and switch tactics.

Even worse is an enthusiastic leasing agent who over exaggerates the property and available units. Since most management companies require units to be market ready before they are shown many times a prospect can't see the unit they are going to rent when they are filling out the application. They are basing their decision on the model and what they are being told by the leasing agent.

The leasing process is the first chance to work resident retention. ALWAYS show the resident the unit that they are going to apply for or make any application contingent upon them seeing the unit. Make sure that they have a chance to see the warts and make their own informed decision.

What you think may be a problem may not be to the prospect but you won't know that until they see the unit. Let the prospect choose to see the unit before the make-ready is completed if they wish. It is better to loose a prospect by being honest than have someone move in and become unhappy and plan on moving as soon as his or her lease expires.

Your Current Residents

A common complaint from many new residents is that they are waited on hand and foot when they first come looking but are ignored once they move in. This should be when resident service really starts. This is when the actual work must begin.

Check back with your residents shortly after they move in and make sure everything is working okay. One popular tactic is to place a six-pack of coke in the fridge along with a gift certificate for a free pizza, napkins and paper plates on the counter. Many times local pizza shops will sell these to you for a discount or even give them to you for free to have the first chance of servicing new residents to the area. This can help make the move in process a little less stressful.

Make sure that there is a refrigerator magnet that has the phone numbers for your office and after hour's emergency maintenance number. Make it easy for the resident to contact you if there are any problems. It will only aggravate the resident if they have to hunt for phone numbers to complain. As part of a safety strategy include fire, ambulance and poison control center numbers on your refrigerator magnet.

Too many apartment communities give lip service to resident retention but only think about it when the resident is getting ready to move. If you wait till then you have missed your best opportunities.

You don't have to do parties or stage cute events. The best thing that you can do for resident retention is to service the hell out of them while they are a resident.

Service them in such a way that they can see a constant good value in their rental dollar and you'll have a resident who won't leave unless they have no choice.

Remember too that your residents will talk to friends and family that also live in other apartments. If you deliver consistent quality service the word will get around and you will receive a ton of referrals from happy residents.

Another thing to consider is an ongoing maintenance program. Why wait until after a resident moves out to upgrade or paint a unit. Many times a resident will move because their unit is getting that lived in look. They see empty units being painted and getting new carpet and appliances. As soon as they move we do the work that could have kept them as residents in the first case.

Why not offer this work to your current residents as a way of retaining current residents. The work will be a little harder and might cost a little more in an occupied unit but in the long run you will gain much more than what you loose.

When They Leave

Even when you get a notice from someone don't give up. That is unless it is someone that you really want to get rid of. Make it a point to contact residents giving notice and express your sadness at their departure.

Always ask why and see if there is anything that you can do to change their mind. Let them know that you don't want them to leave. If it is necessary for them to move you might find out that they are moving to an area where your management company manages properties and to whom you can refer them.

Even if they end up leaving remember that the last impression is the one that they will remember and pass on to others. Will they remember you kindly or be glad they left. Former residents can be a great source of new resident referrals after they move if they are pleased with their stay.

When someone gives notice make sure you have some type of handout delivered that reminds them what his or her duties and yours are. Make sure to remind them about how long it will take to get their deposit back and what they need to do to make sure it is all returned.

You should also give information on what the charges are for the various types of repairs and cleaning. Don't assume that they will remember this from the lease they signed a year or more ago. Treat them fairly and if there is some dispute try your best to negotiate a mutually satisfactory resolution.

Ongoing Strategies

It is important to pay attention to the shifts and trends on your property. If someone is being a little vague about why they are moving or if you have several apartments in the same area giving notice at the same time, it might be time for a little detective work. Check out the apartments in the area and see if one of the neighbors is causing a problem.

Many times someone is playing the stereo too loud or in some other manner disturbing the quiet enjoyment of the other residents. If so, this person or unit will continue to cause you to loose residents and you must deal with them as quickly as possible.

Its like the saying that one bad apple can spoil the whole basket. Well one bad resident can cause a lot of move-outs before the problem becomes obvious so make sure you keep your eyes and ears open. Make sure that your staff is also aware of this policy and is an extension of your efforts.

Ongoing resident surveys should be a part of your retention effort. If you don't ask, many times the resident won't tell you about problems until it is to late to fix them.

You should give surveys to new residents after they move in. While the leasing process is fresh in their mind ask them what they liked and didn't like. Every once in a while ask current residents to take the time and grade your performance. When someone moves out is extremely important to get his or her thoughts.

Equally important is to survey the people that come to your office but don't lease. Why didn't they lease and what were their impressions. What was it that made them rent somewhere else? This can be easily handled with postage paid pre-addressed postcards printed with a few quick questions.

Make sure that you realize that there will be a certain number of harsh criticisms. Keep the big picture in mind. Many times people will only complete these cards if they are upset about something. Look to these cards for ideas but keep them in perspective.

One final note. Something that has always bugged me is the proliferation of the professional property newsletter that is used for resident retention. These slick publications are very professional looking but have little to do with your specific property. Generally the largest part is generic filler with a few choices on articles and a couple spots that are tailored to the property.

If you can't take the time to do something yourself I think it is better to just leave it be. A simple single page double-sided newsletter printed on a copier is much better than the slick sales pieces.

It doesn't even have to be a regular monthly newsletter. Just personalize it to your property needs. Announce work that is being done or being scheduled. Give answers to questions or even seasonal recipes. Have a manager's corner to put in a story or announce policy changes. Have a joke corner where residents can vie for some small prize. Done in a homey amateur style it will always get more attention than some slick piece that looks like everything else your resident gets in the mail.

Also don't do birthdays or new arrivals. In addition to the legal concerns, you will inevitably insult somebody by missing him or her so why take that chance. Don't use the newsletter to complain about residents or things they aren't doing. Those types of things should be handled in a more professional letter to the residents. Always keep the newsletter light and interesting for the residents. Never - never – ever use it as a soapbox to lecture from.

Remember that the newsletter can be a great resident retention tool. Use it to point out all the good things that you are doing for the residents and how hard you and your staff work at creating a good value for them in their home.

Use it to remind them about the resident referral bonuses that you are paying. Tell them about the training that you and your staff are getting to service them even better. When you get a new staff member introduce them in the newsletter. If a current staff member leaves let the residents know they left in your newsletter. Always list the entire staff and their positions. Make sure you list emergency and after hours maintenance numbers along with the normal office hours and numbers.

The most important thing to remember is that every thing that is done on property can be used for resident retention. Always be on the lookout for new ideas on servicing your residents better. Remember though that you cannot do it alone. Make sure your staff is helping and not hindering your efforts.

"Excellence is not an act, but a habit."

--Aristotle--

Chapter Five
Motivate Your Staff To Excellence

"Keep the pearls and toss the swine."

Motivating and empowering your staff should be one of the principal duties for anyone whose job description involves supervising employees. The costs of ignoring this fundamental responsibility can be colossal. Failure in this task not only results in a direct loss in terms of the productivity of your staff and potential lost business, there will also generally be a higher turnover of employees.

Motivation In The Work Place

Employees who aren't motivated won't be productive. It's as simple as that. Yet many of the properties that I have observed had problems with even basic motivation. You could see a direct effect in both how the staff worked and in how they handled the residents and potential residents.

Many times the staff would have the attitude that they were being paid just enough to show up. They would wander from job to job trying to stretch each out for as long as possible before starting another.

This loss of productivity affects everything from how fast work orders are completed to how long unit vacancy turns will take. All these directly impact your bottom financial line.

In addition, people who are unmotivated are unlikely to stay around for very long. They will always be looking for the proverbial greener grass. This means there will be the additional costs of continually replacing and training staff.

There was one property that changed maintenance supervisors five times in a period of two years. Every one of these supervisors was a skilled maintenance person who initially desired to succeed at their job. Yet each one left after a short period of time because of the burnout caused by the general lack of motivation and organization on that property.

Very few companies train their management in the motivation of their staffs. The average property manager is unskilled in motivating his or her staff unless they have taught themselves. In fact even most corporate personnel have only a rudimentary knowledge of motivation and its importance. That is another of the main reasons there is so much turnover at all levels of staff in our industry.

If you ask the typical manager how they motivate some form of pressuring their staff is usually described. Many think that you have to ride roughshod over your staff to get results.

Indeed most manager meetings that I have attended always seem to end up with an us against them attitude. How do we (the managers) make them (the maintenance, leasing, cleaning staffs) do a better job?

Most managers feel that since their staff are being paid money to work that they should work without any further motivation. Even when bonuses are given they are generally used so poorly that they discourage the employee. How to motivate your staff is a highly charged yet vital subject that every successful manager must address.

One of the problems is that the business world we live in has changed so dramatically. To be a successful supervisor, it is extremely important to continue attracting and retaining quality staff. The bottom line is that you are only as good as the people who work for you. But it can be an uphill battle.

A recent survey by the Wilson Learning Corporation found that nearly 80% of today's employees feel passive about their work. They won't consider doing extra work and are content to just get by.

Another survey says that nearly 40% of employees don't trust their supervisors. If four out of ten employees are busy watching their back, who does that leave servicing the customer.

Without trust employee morale plummets and productivity suffers. When employees can't trust their supervisors it will also create an extremely stressful workplace.

With an estimated 50-60% of employee absenteeism due to stress in the workplace this is an issue that cannot be ignored.

The Supervisors Role In Motivation

An organization can be no better than the opinion that its employees hold of it. An upbeat work environment and high employee morale can make positive things happen.

More than any other person on a property, the manager affects the morale and productivity of the people that they supervise. Even when a company is cold and aloof to its employees a good on-site manager can instill pride and loyalty in their staff.

A motivated staff will support your goals and help you by accomplishing their job with a minimum of supervision. The work environment will become less stressful and a lot more work will be accomplished.

In case of an emergency project a motivated staff will be more willing to go that extra mile to make sure the work gets completed. Morale is best when there is a prevailing mood of cooperation and human concern combined with the visible support and trust of your co-workers. It is not based solely on the wages paid.

Historically property management companies have managed in a hierarchy like most other businesses. Any decisions that needed to be made were pushed up the chain of command. Then the decision came back down. Sometimes this happened with little or no input from the people who were closest to the situation.

The main problem with this type of decision-making in the current business environment is it slows down the decisions that everybody needs to do their job. Consumers today expect quick answers and will not accept delays. Another problem is that it takes the power to make decisions away from the people that are closest to the customer and have the best information that is needed to make a good decision.

Empowering Your Staff

Empowering your staff is a huge step towards positively motivating them. To empower your staff you need to do the opposite of what most typical companies do. You need to push decisions down to the lowest possible level. Whenever possible they need to be made by the people that are directly dealing with your customers.

Another of the first steps in making empowerment work requires you to do something that is unnatural for most managers. You need to share information with your staff. In a hierarchical organization information is kept under lock and key. An employee will only know when they do something wrong. You need to flip this process to succeed. In today's world you need to share information widely with your entire staff.

Many managers and a lot of supervisors use the mushroom theory of employee management. Keep them in the dark and feed them a lot of bullshit. This will do nothing but destroy the motivation and moral of your staff.

You don't have to let your staff in on every single thing that is happening at the property, but you do need to let them know everything that affects their job and how they do it.

When an employee understands the reasons behind a policy or process they will be able to better understand the need for it. It will also motivate them to act responsibly in situations because they better understand the full effects of their actions.

It also lets your staff see the current situation or any that arises in clearer terms. This will allow the employees to "buy into" the organization and its goals. Being on the inside loop will empower your employees to accept more responsibility for their performance and contributions to the results of your team as a whole.

Surveys recently done in the US and the UK by Mercers show that employees distrust the companies that they work for. Only 34% of US workers agreed with a statement that they could trust the managers of the company they work for to be honest. Communication is the key to overcoming this problem.

This same survey showed that employee satisfaction along with their commitment and intention to stay is closely tied to how successfully their employer communicates with them.

Sharing information will also become a two way street. When giving information you need to be open to feedback from your staff. There is a wealth of information and ideas that your staff has that can be used to make your job and theirs much easier. Don't be the kind of manager that always has to be right. Always be open to ideas and criticisms. Your staff is your eyes and ears on property. Make sure that you use them.

To start your staff down the road to empowerment you will need to set some goals and create new ways for them to achieve them. Whenever you can you need to lead by example. Any manager that is willing to step up and try new things is a manager that the staff will appreciate and follow. Nobody wants to work for a do as I say not as I do type of manager.

An extremely important part of this new process is to allow your staff to learn even if they make a mistake. Taking chances and sometimes failing is the road to excellence. If your staff is expected to never make mistakes they will be locked in mediocrity. They will never experiment and grow.

Once you set the boundaries for what is expected from each staff member you need to step out of the way and allow them to stretch their wings.

Human nature is such that when it encounters something new and unknown it will try to look for the safety of the familiar. However, once your employees know that they will not get into trouble for trying something new they will blossom into a creative juggernaut.

Just give them the safety of some good parameters and goals along with a clear understanding of their responsibilities and they'll make your job much easier.   Make sure that your communications are always open and working.

Answer questions but make sure that your staff knows that they are expected to be part of the problem solving process. Require that your staff bring you options when they come to ask about problems. Nothing will chew up time faster than having a staff that is always asking you to solve every little problem. Empower them by making them part of the process and moral will soar.

The sad fact is that most managers are much better at critiquing employees than complimenting. To begin with remember the basic rule is that you should always criticize in private and compliment in public.

Then to empower the employee you need to make sure they understand why what they did was wrong and what the effect is on them, you and the big picture.

Then take it even further and ask yourself if this is an issue that other workers might not understand and if so explain it to them as clearly as possible.

Knowledge is a powerful weapon, but knowledge in the right place at the right time is exponentially more powerful.   By keeping your workers in the information loop you will allow them to become one of your most powerful assets.

Your team will come alive when everyone sees where his or her effort contributes to the big picture. Everyone must know the effect their job has on the scheme of things.

You will be amazed at what happens when your team starts to form. Instead of being in competition with each other they will support and help each other learn, grow and complete their duties. Your staff will become more fluid and responsive to the needs of the group as situations change.

It never ceases to amaze me the things that I hear when I talk to various managers about their property staffs. It seems that most managers must have never had a really good motivated staff work for them and have no idea how to manage the ones that they do have. Either that or they would realize how many problems they cause for themselves.

Inferior work problems always start at the top. By accepting poor work, missed deadlines and excuses managers set the tone for the work standards. While there is such a thing as a bad employee in most cases your employees will work up or down to the level that you accept. You'll never know what your staff is capable of unless you raise that bar.

Every employee has a wealth of knowledge and experience that they can bring to their work. To be a successful manager you need to focus and use this experience.

As both a vendor working on different properties and a property manager I have seen both sides of the coin. I've seen managers that motivate and enlighten their staffs and managers that destroy moral and end up causing huge problems and wondering what happened.

Compensating Your Employees

Of course money is one of the biggest compensations for working. Don't make the mistake of thinking that it is the only one though. Other factors of importance include job security, advancement opportunities, benefits, praise, recognition, trust and or the challenges of the job.

Satisfaction in the work they are doing is a huge motivator. In surveys many employees place job satisfaction at nearly the same level as the money rewards.

While many companies use some type of bonuses in an attempt to motivate their staffs' caution must be used. Use bonuses to reward for behavior that you desire. Bonuses must be clearly defined and easy to understand. Bonuses that are hard to understand or are overly complicated will backfire.

Make sure that any bonuses are paid as close to the action that is being rewarded as possible. Make sure that your staff clearly understands the way to earn the bonuses and exactly when they will be paid. Remember that the closer the reward is to the action the more powerful the motivation to repeat the action will be.

Yet according to Alfie Kohn, and echoed by many other organizational gurus, money can actually become a disincentive to production. In his *New York Times* article "For Best Results, Forget the Bonus," Kohn writes, "While rewards are effective at producing temporary compliance, they are strikingly ineffective at producing lasting changes in attitudes or behavior."

There have also been about two dozen studies in the field of social psychology that seem to prove that people who expect to receive a reward do not perform as well as those who expect nothing."

The bottom line seems to be that money needs to be combined with other types of rewards to best motivate your staff. Clear communication with and from employees will help you to create the best mix for your staff.

This same idea should be used for the entire payroll. Make sure to clearly communicate the pay scales to your employees. For example, all maintenance staff has various experience levels. A clearly defined pay structure tied to the type of experience that a person brings to their job will be a strong motivator for improvement. It will also clearly show an employee what they need to do to advance in rank and pay.

A maintenance person in training might begin as a Maintenance Tech I. Someone with more experience would be at Maintenance Tech II. It could then go through several more experience levels to Maintenance Supervisor Level I. The number of levels required would depend upon the companies' needs and size of the staffs.

Each level would have a specific pay range. Each would have a specific set of skills required along with the ways that these skills would be tested. The skills might include classes or on the job experience. A modifier would be used to reward longer lengths time on the job. The longer a person works for you the more they should be paid.

Many companies require that employees not discuss what they are paid. Assuming that people will not talk to each other about what they are being paid is naive. It is much better to have a clear easy to understand pay scale.

It is also typical that employees are evaluated once per year and any increases awarded at that time. To motivate your employees you must scrap this antiquated system.

Setting up a clear route that employees must follow to successfully pass through each pay scale will allow the employee to have an input into what they want to be paid. It is not based only on an arbitrary evaluation by their supervisor but also on their own efforts to improve themselves.

As soon as an employee qualifies for a new level they should be paid at that level. Each time there is a position open on one of your properties it can be posted with pay scale and requirements.

By having people paid on a uniform pay scale it can be used company wide and even modified quarterly to motivate your staff. Bonuses should then be tied to specific property financial or operational goals.

Using a uniform scale of experience will allow properties to transfer and promote staff with the knowledge they are getting the skills that they require.

Know Your Staff And Property

Empowering your staff does not mean you allow employees to do as they wish. You need to get out there and see what is going on around your property. Call it management by wandering around.

At different times during different days you need to wander around to the places your staff is supposed to be working. You need to wander in and see just what they are doing. You're not doing this to find people doing things wrong, you're doing this to find people doing things right.

When you find somebody doing something wrong, and you will, keep your cool and respond as calmly as you can. You are trying to create a trusting and cooperative work atmosphere, not find problems.

When you find people doing things right you need to compliment them, preferably when their fellow workers are around. Raise the bar on your expectations and watch your team blossom.

Several things will be accomplished by doing this. Once your staff gets used to you surprising them they will tend to remain on their toes because you just might show up at anytime. It will also show them that you are interested in them and their problems. It will allow and encourage them to give you feedback in a more private setting.

When you go out on property and the turf that is generally left to your staff you are making yourself much more accessible. One affect is that your staff can ask you questions and show you the options while you are right there instead of wasting time coming into the office and trying to describe what you need to know.

As important is that it will help you get a much better handle on what is being done along with how much time different tasks should take. Nothing upsets a staff member more than to be at the wrong end of unreasonable expectations.

Make it your job to know how long things should take to accomplish. Don't just tell your staff member how long it should take, ask them. If their estimate seems out of sync with yours ask them why?

An important philosophy that you need to learn is that you should always set people up to succeed. This is an extremely simple but powerful concept. Make sure that both you and your staff member have reasonable expectations on how long a task will take and you are setting them up to succeed.

This will also help you realize when someone is not working up to his or her full potential and you can question him or her about the reasons why. A lot of times all that is needed are some extra training or tools. What's more it will let you see when someone is doing superior work for you.

Finally, being out on the property will allow you to feel the pulse of the property and get a jump on potential problems while they are still small. Carry a radio or pad with you to note what you see that needs attention.

To create and maintain good communications with your workers it is very important for you to take the time and be available to listen to your staff. If someone asks to talk to you at a time when you are busy, make sure you schedule a time to get together with him or her as soon as possible.

Try to schedule a specific time and place so they know you are interested in hearing them out. Then make sure that you listen. If you don't know the answer to their question tell them you will check it out and get back to them. Then make sure that you do so.

If it is questions of policy make sure that they understand fully why the policy exists and how it affects and helps them. If they are unhappy about something see if you can help.

You also need to know the difference between helping and interfering. Once you empower your staff you need to learn to step back and get out of the way. The whole goal for empowering staff is to allow them to make your job easier. Failure to allow them to stand on their own two feet will destroy your effort from the beginning.

Another positive thing that you can do is celebrate when you have completed a significant goal or accomplished an extra hard task you and your staff have been working on. It can be as simple as a pizza lunch, an employee barbeque or donuts and fresh coffee when they report to work in the morning.

When you are having one of these celebrations make sure that you explain why you are doing it and how each worker shared in the triumph. Make it fun. Above all else, absolutely no criticizing should be allowed.

Have periodic meetings whenever there is a new goal or when a new staff member joins you. Never finish any meeting whether it is with an individual that reports to you or with your entire staff without asking if there are any issues or problems that anyone needs to address. This can be extremely difficult and uncomfortable but needs to be done.

If there is a problem you need to know about it before it grows. Allowing your staff the freedom to question without fear of censure will keep many problems small.

Always address any problem brought up openly and honestly. Sometimes there are things that you just can't fix, that are out of your hands. But many things can be solved simply if you find out about them early enough.

Most on site meetings should be between you and your staff. Discourage your supervisor from attending. It will likely kill the freedom that your staff would feel in asking you questions or telling you about their thought on problems and issues.

If necessary you can contact your supervisor later and find out the answer to questions. Always watch yourself. Make sure that you are open and honest and don't use these meetings to target or berate anyone and your staff will start to trust you and form a team.

NEVER EVER allow a supervisor to directly criticize one of your staff.   Nothing will destroy an employee's moral faster than allowing that to happen.   If you are the manager you must accept responsibility for everything that happens on your property.   If a supervisor starts to criticize one of your staff you need to step in and deflect as much as possible.   This may get you in a little hot water but ultimately it will have the affect of solidifying your team and their trust.

If someone on your staff has done something wrong you can deal with him or her later in private.   You need to be a buffer between your supervisors and your staff.   If a supervisor has a problem with a member of your staff you need to be clear that it is your property and you want them to go through you.

At the same time **NEVER-EVER-EVER** accept any compliment as solely yours whether anyone else from your staff is there or not.   Always make sure that you receive any compliments as a team accomplishment.

If you only extend the compliment to your staff when they are around it will end up sounding fake when you do.   Only if you truly believe and make sure and share all the compliments will you come across as sincere.   Make sure that whether the compliment is from a supervisor or resident that it gets passed around.

If you have never managed like this before it will take time for your staff to understand, accept and believe that you are willing to listen to their ideas and complaints. Keep at it though and the results will astound you.

Another vital policy is to allow and encourage your staff to question instructions if they don't understand or agree with them. Even though you are their supervisor you won't always know what is the best way to do things and pretending that you do will only make you look stupid. Always be open to listening for new and better ideas or suggestions. You can't be everywhere at once and need the team to work together to find the best ways to accomplish its goals.

It is equally important when you do get an idea from a staff member to always make sure to give them credit. You'll be astounded at how many good ideas your staff can come up with if you let them. That is empowering.

Always remember that one of your employees' greatest motivators is their pride. Remember that and work hard to create a work environment that your staff can take pride in.

The Importance Of Retaining Your Staff

The bottom line is that the only good reason to loose a good staff member is if they get promoted. Other than that your goal should be to keep them happy, motivated and working for you. To do so you must know where and what they want to do. If it is within your power to help make sure you do so.

By retaining and empowering your staff you will also have the beginning of a powerful resident retention program. Resident retention and employee retention are closely tied together.

To make both strategies work your staff must clearly understand the benefits to them. These benefits need to be constantly and continually pointed out.

Our industry has an especially huge turnover of employees at the property level. People in our business are constantly changing jobs and moving on looking for something better.

Lack of continuity of property staff is one largely overlooked factor in the big picture. Every time a staff member leaves they also take a wealth of experience and contacts in your community with them.

If a manager at a fast food restaurant costs more than $30,000 in lost income and training costs to replace how much would an apartment manager cost? The higher the position and the more specialized the training that is required the more the cost to replace that staff member.

These costs include actual recruiting cost like advertising and fees for tests and referrals. Supervisors must divert time to interviewing and checking references.

Even when the new staff member is hired the costs will continue. Each new staff member must be trained. Any ongoing projects are either stopped or slowed down while the new staff member comes up to speed.

Getting to know a new staff and residents can take a manager several months. Meanwhile there is a direct loss of knowledge, decreased morale, and increases in employee stress that will affect the production of every other member of the staff.

On a very practical level, even new maintenance staff member must spend a lot of time learning about the layout of the property and its specific problems. Just knowing where supplies and materials are stored and which keys open what can be challenging.

Heating and cooling systems are unique from property to property. There is no way to standardize the supplies needed to repair sinks and other plumbing fixtures. Learning this is time that they will not be serving your residents or turning vacancies. Staff that has been on a property for an extended period of time will also have historical memories about repairs, incidents and residents that simply can't be duplicated. All these will disappear as soon as they leave.

A good example happened one time when I had been transferred to a new property. I still lived on the original property for a few weeks after the transfer. A new manager and leasing agent had been hired at my old property.

I had gone into the office one weekend to pick up a package that had been delivered when I overheard the leasing agent receiving a call from an irate resident about not having any hot water. The boilers had shut off and both the hot water and heat were down.

The leasing agent was trying to explain that a heating contractor had been called and would be there as soon as they could. When she hung up I asked if they had tried to hit the reset button on the boiler. I had watched one time when the boiler repairperson was showing the maintenance supervisor how to restart the boiler.

Since the maintenance supervisor had been transferred with me no one on the property knew about the reset button. I offered to try and see if that was the problem. Five minutes later the boiler had been restarted and everybody started to calm down. This one five minute incident saved the property several hundred dollars in weekend rate vendor costs.

The bottom line is that literally thousands of dollars of unnecessary expenses occur when an experienced staff member is transferred or lost. Remember that the only good reason to loose a staff member is if they are being promoted.

Another key argument for employee retention is that having staff members that the resident recognizes makes them feel more comfortable on your property. It makes it easier for the resident to communicate any problems and know that it will be taken care of by someone they know and trust.

It is extremely important to show your staff how important their contacts with residents are to the big picture and empower them to satisfy your residents whenever possible. Being able to deliver excellent service is an easy way to build the pride of your staff.

Every staff member should also be encouraged to always be looking for ways to deliver superior service. A part of doing this is encouraging every staff member to start looking at any complaint as a first step in finding another way to deliver that superior service.

It is inevitable that things will be overlooked or accidents happen. Residents will typically try to talk to the first staff member that they see if they feel they are being ignored. Teaching your staff how to deal with these situations and turn them into a positive encounter is something that will take time but is extremely important.

Once you have taught your staff to accept any unhappy resident as a challenge they will really start to build pride in both you and your property. You have to invest a lot of time in molding your staff into a well-oiled motivated team but it will pay back with huge future returns.

How you prioritize work orders is an easy way to start your staff down the path of empowerment.   It can also be used for resident retention. As an example ask yourself and your staff how often a resident will approach a maintenance person in the halls. They have a problem that they want to have fixed.

If your staff member tells them they need to call the office they are clearly telling the resident that they have something more important to take care of than that resident. An incredibly good impression can be made if your maintenance people handle this contact differently.

Since every property of any size has radios or phones for the maintenance staff they should use them. All your staff has to do is take a quick look at the residents' problem and report it while the resident is still standing there. Your staff can see what supplies they will need to fix the problem and that will save them time later.

The office can also confirm the request along with prioritizing and scheduling a work order. Many problems only take a few minutes to fix and can be easily done when they are called to your attention. Most important to the resident is that you to take the time to help them. This is the way you keep your residents and create pride in your workers.

As your maintenance staff completes each work order it should be looked at as an opportunity. Your staff should be constantly trained to use these occasions to provide superior service your residents. Whenever a maintenance person goes into an apartment to do a work order they should always be trained to ask and look for other unreported problems that they can fix.

Whether it is as simple as a loose doorknob or as complicated as a major leak - your staff needs to be on the lookout for these golden opportunities.

Not only should they be looking for broken things but also for other chances to keep your resident happy. They can see a dirty carpet that you can offer to clean or a touch up on paint from a repair. Over time you can also train them to recognize other opportunities. Good service like this will decrease both apartment turnover and work orders in general.

Many times a problem that can be easily handled early on will become much more complex and time consuming if allowed to continue. This is especially true of water leaks.

Training your staff to react this way will create positive feedback from your residents. Hearing and receiving this feedback is a very important part in instilling your staff with a sense of pride in their property, their work and fellow workers.

Everyone on your staff must buy into the concept of superior service and be empowered to deliver it. Even more, they must look for every opportunity to show their pride and support of each other in their jobs. A friendly staff that is always looking for an opportunity to give such superior service will make it easy to keep occupancy high and turnover low in any market.

TEN WAYS TO KEEP YOUR BEST EMPLOYEES MOTIVATED AND HAPPY:

1. Criticize in private / compliment in public

2. Make sure your staff has all the information they need to do their job.

3. Make sure they have needed tools.

4. Insulate your staff from your supervisors.

5. Empower your staff to make decisions.

6. Keep employee turnover down.

7. Make the customer key.

8. Treat your staff as good or better than your customers.

9. Listen to your staff.

10. Always make it a team effort

"If you have an important point to make, don't try to be subtle or clever. Use a pile driver. Hit the point once. Then come back and hit it again. Then hit it a third time a tremendous whack."

--Winston Churchill--
[British WWII Prime Minister]

Chapter Six
Leasing Made Simple

"Why work harder than you need to?"

The simple bottom line is that leasing can be as hard or as easy as we make it. When we lease an apartment we become a salesperson. Successful sales require a process be followed to complete the transaction. The important thing is to customize this process in a way that you will be comfortable with.

Our customers are looking for rental housing and the services that go along with it. All we have to do is price the unit so that people will find value in it and our owners will have a fair return on their money.

What Type Of Sales

Nearly everyone who leases apartments has been trained in some type of program that instructs its participants on the sales process.

Many of these train leasing agents to ask leading questions that will take your prospect down the road until the only answer left is yes when you ask if they want to lease. Some leasing people even take pride in the fact that they have learned to do a hard close. Yet that type of selling is at least twenty years out of date and our industry is one of the few that still use it.

At the other end of the spectrum is the agent who simply shows you the apartment and answers questions that you have. They never even try to market their apartments. I've even had a few agents that seemed content with handing me the keys to the apartment and telling me where to go.

Some type of sales process is obviously required but the hard closing is passé. Most professional sales people have moved on to some type of solution based selling where they are assisting the prospect in making their decision and not trying to trap them.

The first thing that we must realize is that a lot of the people we are leasing to have had their own sales training. They know what a sales spiel looks like and we're not fooling them.

They understand the process as we attempt to get them to agree to small things so we can pop the big question. While a few people may fall for these tactics most of our prospects really don't like this type of sales pressure.

The amazing thing is that we lease as much as we do using these types of arm-twisting hard sale tactics. A lot of times we seem to lease our apartments in spite of ourselves.

Another major point is that while a few people are comfortable with this type of selling the majority of leasing people are not and have trouble doing their job because of this type of hard sale. They are so busy trying to remember all the things they have been trained that they are "required" to say that they don't have time to listen to the prospect.

Mystery Shoppers

Making it even worse is the way many property management companies use mystery shoppers to check up on their leasing staff. These shoppers will come into a property office with a checklist of items they are looking for. They mark off each item as the leasing agent covers it.

Since the leasing agent doesn't find out till much later when they have had a mystery shopper there is no way that they could remember what was going on that specific day. Many times the results of these shops are used in determining whether the leasing person is doing a good job. Using mystery shoppers in this way will only annoy your staff.

What is amazing is that a property management company will use someone they don't know, whom they didn't train to evaluate their staff. While using a mystery shopper to look at broad strokes may work, the time and money would be better used in training their staff.

The best way to train people has always been with immediate feedback. At the minimum the shoppers should identify themselves upon completion of the tour so the leasing agent can understand the grading they are getting.

Bottom line though, these are random checks and should never be used for determining how well a leasing person is doing his or her job. There are enough quantifiable ways to accomplish this without using the input of an unverifiable third person report.

One manager that I know even had a mystery shopper come on property that was belligerent. Ultimately this manager kicked the shopper off the property. The shopper wrote a scathing report that was used at the managers' next review as a way to deny them a pay increase.

Star Leasing

If you check the star leasers they typically are the people who have personalized the sales process. They work outside of the box of what they are required to do. They don't memorize a spiel that is the same for every prospect. They listen to their prospects and customize their presentation on the fly.

Listening is the main key to the entire sales process. You would think that the typical sales agent really liked the sound of their voice as they try to work in every benefit that they can think off into the conversation.

By listening to our prospect they will tell us exactly what it is that they are looking for in an apartment. They will tell us what they like and what they don't like. We just have to listen and ask a few questions here and there.

I always trained my leasing agents that they were allowed to ask one question for every question that the prospect asked. Otherwise the prospect feels like you are grilling them and they put up defenses. Always ask leading questions to encourage the prospect to expand on their answer and give you more insight.

Most leasing agents tend to be a little uncomfortable with the whole sales process. They constantly receive pressure from their manager or supervisor to close a certain percentage of prospects as leases.

It helps to think of leasing in terms of a steak and the sizzle as it cooks. All properties are basically leasing boxes that are their apartments. In the same price range and geographic area apartments tend to look remarkably similar. One of the main things that we are really selling is the sizzle.

This sizzle is any added value that the prospect perceives that is coming with that box. In general sizzle consists of what type of lifestyle the prospect feels they will have if they rent one of your boxes.

The sizzle is created in the minds of your prospects by a large number of rapid impressions that they receive during their initial contacts with you. It will include input from your advertising, location, how the phone is answered, curb appeal, leasing office, greeting from your staff, the presentation at your property, and many other factors.

To begin fine-tuning your leasing process you need to first understand the basic profile of the people that are already living on your property. This profile will involve information on income level, where they work, how they found you, what things they consider most and least popular about your property and other factors.

Often we try to market to too large a market. Remember that when we are marketing apartments we are basically selling a service. The marketing of a service and a product are two totally different things. For one thing marketing of products doesn't have to deal with fair housing laws.

When you set up a profile you need to be careful not to cross the lines of fair housing and use common sense. Information that you can use is based on job types, initial source of prospect and income level. Go to far beyond these and you risk brushing against the gray areas of fair housing. This is something that you don't need or want to do.

Once you understand your current residents you can then decide if you are trying to maintain this basic profile or want to upgrade it.

One important thing to watch is where your residents who lease are coming to you from. What are the advertising sources that they used? Make the distinction between the people who just stop by and the people who actually end up leasing from you.

Accumulate this information for both just your current residents and a compilation of your historical data. When you compare these two you might see interesting connections between the results and advertising.

You should also watch your competitors to see where they are advertising. Keep in mind though that just because you see advertising in a certain media doesn't mean that it is working for your rival properties.

Every property has a specific character and appeal for its residents. Whether it is based on location, style, age or price any marketing that takes these factors in mind will be more successful.

Using this information you can create a marketing plan to draw in more qualified prospects. The key to any plan is finding those qualified prospects that lease and not just shoppers.

Any marketing plan should include paid advertising, promotional efforts, property advertising and any other strategy that you want to use.

When you are thinking of print advertising remember that you should be comparing your ads to your competition. Design your advertising with a consistent approach and design. Does yours stand out? Does it give the information that a prospect needs to find your property and show how they can get their questions answered?

Make sure that you include using technology to market. A dedicated fax on demand line where people can get copies of floor plans, pricing and policies can be useful and is easy to set up.

Web sites are also becoming more and more useful. During the recent technology downturns interest in this type of marketing has fallen but it can still be highly useful. The number of people that are using the Internet continues to increase every day.

This use will become more pervasive as the Internet interfaces become increasingly user friendly, prices lower and connections easier and faster.

Using the Internet you can easily include masses of information that would not be affordable by any other means. The prospect can pick and choose what they are interested in seeing based on their needs.

A web site should include floor plans, policies, and pictures of the community, virtual tours, applications and information on the benefits your community has to offer.

Don't stop there. Include a copy of your latest newsletter, pictures of resident functions, pictures of your staff working and information on any recent training or awards they received. Make sure to include maps to the property and information on how to contact your office.

Small publications and newspapers that are printed for specific audiences and groups in your area can be an economical source of prospects. These will tend to be much less expensive than the major daily newspapers on a per lease basis.

Curb Appeal

A primary key area that you will need to focus on is the curb appeal of your property. Every once in a while you need to drive past your property and see how it looks.

It is important to be honest and blunt. Do the buildings and grounds look clean and well kept? Are the curbs and signs neatly and freshly painted? Is the leasing office easy to find? Is there parking easily available for prospects? Try and look at your property like a prospect. Try to imagine what they will see when they drive by. Is it the type of place that will appeal to your prospects?

This will be the first chance to show off your property to your prospect. Whether they are coming because of an ad or phone conversation with someone in the office it is critical to make this first impression a good one.

Ask friends, family and colleagues for their input. What are their impressions of your property? Here again you should try to create an individual spin. You should not be trying to look the same as every other property around you.

One area that you can easily customize is with your landscaping. Instead of the same flowers as everyone else try different sizes and colors. Make sure to purchase plants that flower at different times during the season and are perennials so you won't have to replace them every year.

Another way to stand out is to keep all your exterior signs and curbs freshly painted and clean. Make sure one of the first things every day is to clean the entryway into your office.

Current Residents

It is important to realize that your current residents can be a significant marketing source. Resident referrals are as good a gold when you are looking for new residents. Who knows better than your current residents about the great service that you offer? Who else knows what a great place and what a super value your apartments are? They are already sold on you. Do you think that these residents live in a vacuum? Of course not, they know all sorts of people who might look for an apartment at one time or another.

Word-of mouth advertising like this may be the most powerful tool that you can use. According to YANKELOVICH MONITOR, which tracks consumer trends more than 70% of consumers consider their family and friends as top sources for advice on new products and services.

A resident referral is as close as to a slam-dunk lease as you can get. When a current resident tells someone how good of a job you are doing at keeping him or her happy it carries much more weight than anything you could possibly say to someone walking into your office. These residents are their friends, family or colleagues. That gives them automatic credibility.

You can encourage referrals by using a resident referral fee to reward your residents who refer new prospects to your property. I've even seen properties that vary the amount monthly based on their number of vacancies.

Frankly I think this just might confuse your residents. They won't understand why the same action is worth more or less during different periods so a set fee should be used. Whether the prospect rents or not you should make sure to thank the resident that refers them. They tried to help you and that type of positive activity needs to be acknowledged and reinforced.

Remember one thing with resident referrals though. As with anything else the closer the reward is to the action the more effective the motivation is to repeat the action.

In other words pay a resident referral fee and pay it quickly. The fastest way will always be a rental credit on the residents account. However, most companies will want to have some sort of tracking and cross check system in place. This will usually include some sort of paperwork that will create an audit trail. Then a check will be issued. Resist this route if you can.

I understand that an authorization procedure needs to be in place to guarantee that only legitimate rental referral fees are getting paid. However, most accounts payable departments work on a net thirty schedule. At best the process will drag out for at least several weeks before the resident gets paid their fee.

The problem with this is that if a referral fee takes longer than a week or two at most to deliver to the resident it can become more of a problem than a reward.

Your resident is on the side of the fence where they have to pay their rent by a specific date or risk late fees. Generally they will not understand why they have to wait for their money. Once the referral moves in the resident should have the fee paid in short order.

The longer a resident has to wait for a referral fee the less value that it has and the less the resident will be motivated to refer someone again. If you are not going to pay referral fees in a timely manner, don't even bother with trying to use them as an incentive.

Every time you drive down a street you are sure to see a sign saying, "rent special today". If you use these make sure that it is today only. Many potential prospects will drive by your property a number of times before they have the time to stop. Seeing the same signs day after day imply that you are desperate for renters.

When someone calls for information listen to how the phone is answered by your staff. There is nothing more fake than some long canned greeting that is the same for every call. Remember that you are much more than a leasing office. You are also a management office.

I recommend that you answer in a friendly manner and identify both your property and yourself. People sense sincerity on the phone. The goal of any phone call should be to entice the prospect to stop at your property. Don't make the mistake of answering questions that they don't ask. Prospects will usually open with the statement that they are looking for some information. The worst mistake that you can make is to start to spout all sorts of information they may not be interested in. The best thing that has always worked for me is to ask the prospect what questions you can answer for them.

You just don't know what a person's buttons are that early in a contact. Answer their questions simply and honestly. Invite them to stop by your property for a tour but don't try to trap them into a commitment. Make sure that the conversation is light and helpful. Make sure to stand out from your competition by being helpful and not pressuring them.

Once a prospect comes onto your property you need to continue this tactic. Your staff needs to focus on helping the prospect by answering the questions that they ask. A good rule was that for every question the prospect asked you are allowed to ask one back. Use your questions to explore the motivations and priorities of the prospect. This will give you an insight into how well your property would fill their needs.

The goal should be for each leasing person to present the information that the prospect needs to be able to make an informed decision.

In many ways the selling environment that most properties seem to strive for is similar to that of a used car lot. The next time you drive past apartments, check out how many have balloons and the small lawn signs. When you go into the office you are latched onto by a professional salesperson who's only goal is to get the prospect to fill out an application and collect a deposit.

You can sell some residents that way but I would argue that you are virtually guaranteeing a huge turnover of residents if you do. The more a property depends upon "sales" to get people into their units the more often these will be the people that will move as soon as their lease is up.

The residents who tend to stay are the people who have decided that the community offers the lifestyle that they desire. This is true because in reality, people really do know what they want.

Your leasing staff should be trained to listen to your prospects. The best salespersons always tend to listen more than they talk.

The bottom line is the prospect already knows what they want. We should be trying to satisfy those wants for them. By listening to every thing the prospect tells us and using questions to determine how well our property satisfies their needs we can help them determine whether or not our property will work for them. In the end though, they must make the final decision.

A well-organized leasing office should also have information on all the properties in the area just in case the prospect is truly adamant that they need some amenity that is not available on your property. Your leasing agents should help direct them to a property that does have what they need.

Go so far as to call the other property and ask what they have available for lease. Give the prospect the directions to get there.

Time after time I did this for prospects and more often than not they would return as soon as they looked at the other property. The leasing staffs at those properties were often my best leasing tools. After being greeted in a cordial and friendly atmosphere at my property they would walk into the competitors office.

Generally these people would immediately start to try and sell the prospect. This happened at the competitors' property while their experience at ours was still fresh in their mind.

Listen to the prospect and they will tell you exactly what they need and are looking for. We should be there to try to facilitate them getting the information they need to make their decision, not twist their arm into deciding to rent at our property. If our apartments don't supply what they need then we should be willing to help them by directing them to a property that will.

Neiman Marcus became one of the most successful retailers in the world by stressing that type of customer service. The job was focused on satisfying the customer, not selling them what you have.

Make the customer feel good and you'll always be ahead. Whether they end up leasing from you or not they will remember the way that you treated them.

 When you handle a prospect in such a helpful and open way they will have no choice but wonder just how well you treat your actual residents. Just stop and think about it for a minute. By helping the prospect you are showing them exactly how you run your property.

You're proving that you will be there for them when they need it. You show just how different you are from everybody else that they could rent from.

Remember that a box is a box. It is your staff, their attitudes and how you treat people that will set you apart from your competitors.

Power marketing does not mean putting balloons out. It makes me chuckle every time I go by a property that does that. Has anybody ever gotten a lease because they had balloons out tied to the sign? People are either going to notice you or they won't. Balloons are not going to make any difference.

Leasing an apartment is not a spur of the moment type purchase. People don't drive down the street and suddenly go, hey there are some balloons, I need to rent there.

Most of your prospects will first decide what area they want to rent an apartment. Then they will decide on a number of different apartments in that specific area that seems to fill their needs. Then they will start to visit and ask questions.

Other people may stop at your property when they drive by on another errand. In either case the first impression of your property will be based on your street appeal and not balloons.

The signs that are put out that tell what your specials are or what amenities your apartments have are a good way to snag passing people. Don't put out any signs that have some kind of time limit on them. Telling people that today is the only day they can get a discount only works if today is the only day. Having the same "today only" special out for days or weeks looks unprofessional and creates a bad impression.

Use caution when you use specials to lure new residents. It can create a bad impression on your current residents. They will wonder why someone new coming to live at your apartments is more valuable than they are.

The first contact that you will generally have with your prospects will be on the phone. Make sure that you and your staff answers politely with the name of your property and the person who answers. I always hate it when someone answers with a cute pre-canned spiel. When the phone is answered the same way every time it tends to sound cold. Allow your people to answer in a more natural way and the conversation will sound more relaxed and welcoming.

The goal of any conversation with a prospect should be to entice the prospect to come to your property. Hard selling over the phone won't work since people can always agree to anything to get away from you. Let the conversation flow and answer only the questions that you are asked. Don't fall into the trap of answering unasked questions. You can easily bring up things that your prospect hasn't thought about.

Many times people will drive by a property several times before they finally have time to stop. This is especially if they work or know people in the area.

You need to keep an eye on how your property is looking. Walk across the street every once in a while and try to look at it through the eyes of a prospect. In the morning, drive by a couple times and see what impression is given. Is your property really giving the impression that you want it to?

The importance of street appeal cannot be overstressed. It is one of the single most important first impressions that you can influence. There was a family that owned a property in Bettendorf Iowa that I lived in a long time ago. At the time it was the property was over 20 years old.

There was a lot of newer and cheaper stuff in the area. At the time the apartment market was soft because of an economic downturn. Yet this property always had a waiting list of residents. The reason was that the entire operation was first-class.

Every morning the staff spent their first hour out on property cleaning and sweeping the walks and lots. Every two or three years the parking lots were resealed and the striping and curbs were redone every year.

In spring the flowerbeds were full of a variety of flowers and shrubs. The matriarch of the family ran the property with an iron fist. Nothing was allowed to be out of place or less than perfect. She lived on the property and had an eye on everything. Yet her entire staff had been with her for years and residents stayed for years and years.

She truly understood and lived the concept of resident retention and understood what a powerful marketing tool it was.

Marketing Trends

Since so many of our ideas in marketing comes from other sales areas it might be interesting to look at a trend that first showed up in the used car business and is now appearing in home sales.

The trend is that of marketing to people with damaged credit. It is estimated that more than 50% of the adult population has less than one month of income in reserve. Any serious injury or accident will quickly push these people over the edge and into credit problems.

Many people will experience credit problems at some point in their lives. The used car industry was the first to recognize the goldmine in this market group. By approving loans to questionable credit risks they were able to charge premium fees and interest on their loans.

The people who market home mortgages were close behind. By increasing charges it is possible to cover the increased potential loses.

Older apartment communities would be a natural market for this type of person. These older properties are constantly battling newer and better properties. By rating credit scores on a number system it would allow properties to offer different options for its applicants based on their credit scores. The worse the score the higher the deposit and fees charged. Flat out denial might be reserved for the people who have a history of residency problems or certain criminal felonies.

It is important to keep an open mind for new opportunities when marketing an apartment property. Watch other industries for new ideas on sales and marketing.

*A person without a sense of humor
is like a wagon without springs,
jolted by every pebble in the road.*

--Henry Ward Beecher—
[American Writer 1813-1887]

Chapter Seven
Make It Fun

"Fun is what makes the world go round."

Fun at work is the result of a combination of a lot of different factors. Much like a spider web the different attitudes and characteristics cross and intertwine to combine into a cohesive whole that is stronger than the filaments of its parts.

One of the main hindrances to a fun work place in our industry is that we tend to take ourselves much too seriously. Self-important and sometimes pretentious people manage many property offices. These solemn and serious people tend to be rigid and forever serious. Their attitude seems to be that we are here to make money, not to have fun.

Indeed many people would think of fun and humor as a hindrance to completing a job. That fun is something that gets in the way of doing business.

Yet fun is both a powerful energizer and a motivator and even though fun at work might sound counterproductive the advantages can be enormous and far-reaching. Motivated people who have fun at work will be much more productive and creative.

They will also be willing to work longer and harder and able to work together with a team of like-minded individuals to accomplish even more. They will tend to show more loyalty to both their co-workers and to the organization that they work for.

Having fun at work is often just a matter of attitude. It is the result of a conscious or unconscious decision to enjoy life. The people who have fun at work are usually the same people who look for new challenges, have a positive personality and have the ability to laugh at themselves.

It is important to bear in mind that typically it is not the work itself that is fun but rather the relationship the members of a work group have developed to cope with the work, each other and life in general.

Places that discourage fun at work at are always easy to spot. There will never be any laughter. No one will be smiling. The staff will show up for work at the last possible minute and leave at the earliest. Everybody looks out for him or herself and frequently snipe at each other.

If they had a choice, is there really anybody who would choose to work at a job that isn't fun? Since we spend such a huge amount of time at work and our jobs are such a critical part of our self-esteem you would think that making work more enjoyable would be of major importance to both the employee and employer.

Yet how often have you gone into a store or business where the employees seemed like zombies. At most they will respond to questions in monotone grunts and just seem to be putting in their time until the end of their shift. The thought seems to be that we are not here to have fun, but just to make the money that we need and then leave as soon as possible.

This type of employee is certainly not servicing their customers in any but the most marginal of ways. No one would describe this type of employee service as exceptional. In spite of that many businesses still ignore the dispositions of their work staff.

While some businesses can survive while supplying this poor of service to their customers, any business that is hoping for repeat business or an ongoing business relationship must do much better.

Grocery stores are one place where you often seem to run into a lot of employees with an unhappy attitude. Many times the clerks are just short of rude and will talk to you as little as possible.

Yet at one local grocery store there is a clerk that is just the opposite. Every time you go into the store you can tell which register she is running. It will always be the one with the longest line. She has something nice to say to every person that comes through her line. It could be about the weather or something that she notices about them. People are willing to stand the extra minutes in her line because she makes them feel special and welcome.

A friend of mine went through her line and she commented on how nice her broach she was wearing was. The broach was a family heirloom and had been given to her by her favorite grandmother. Needless to say it made my friends day.

The neat thing about this clerk is that you can feel how genuinely she enjoys talking to the people in her line.

I'm sure that her days fly by because she allows herself to enjoy the moment and rise above the drudgery of her job. Even though many of the other people in the same store are locked in unhappiness she rises above it. She does this with no apparent help from her manager. We could all learn a lot from her example of how much happier we all could be with a positive attitude. Plus it dramatically impacts her job performance.

Unfortunately, many supervisors believe that you can't have fun and be productive at the same time. Nothing could be further from the truth. Just because someone is laughing doesn't mean that they are not working and being productive.

Social scientists even believe that there is an evolutionary reason that humor and our sense of fun developed. They believe that it developed to allow us to better handle stress.

Humor is one of the things that help us deal with change. It allows us to remain flexible and deal with stressful situations. Most of us are pretty conservative in how we handle unknown circumstances. Humor can be an important tool that helps us handle the stress and changes that are often a part of our daily lives.

Our body even responds physically when we laugh. Our tolerance for pain increases, our heart and pulse rates go up, and we produce chemicals that help with stress response.

In a recent article "Fortune Magazine" identified peak performers in some of the fastest growing companies in America. Then it asked these peak performers what kind of workplace they would be most reluctant to leave. Fully 74%

responded that it would be an environment that promotes fun and a closer working relationship with their colleagues.

In another survey high school students were asked by the Families and Work Institute to rate the most important thing they would look for in a job. A huge majority, 76% answered that they wanted a job that was fun. It was even more important than pay or a challenging work environment.

Three out of four American workers are currently dissatisfied with or fundamentally disconnected from their jobs according to a recent survey completed by the Gallup Management Journal.

In order to succeed as a property manager you need to attract peak performers for your staff. Indeed you need to become one yourself. Every manager needs to recognize the value of fun in attracting successful staff in today's workplace environment.

Fun happens spontaneously. It is not something that can be easily planned and structured. Don't try to segment and plan fun as an activity. You can create time and situations where fun can happen but you can't force it.

Fun should not be about bringing playtime into work. It doesn't involve games or toys to amuse you and your staff. What it does involve is a positive attitude that uses humor as a tool to bond with your fellow workers and deal with the stress of the work environment.

Like the grocery clerk above, if you decide to look for the positive in your work you can also find the fun. You can create an atmosphere where you can enjoy your work. More importantly you can infect your fellow workers with this same healthy attitude.

Nobody would argue that working in property management is necessarily a fun job. It can be rewarding, challenging and profitable, but rarely would you use the word fun to describe it. Yet for the right passionate person, there is fun to be found in any job.

Creating achievable challenges at work are one of the things that can inspire workers to become passionate about their work. The best challenges need to involve tasks where we can use our initiative and imagination. They need to involve the staff in projects where they see themselves and their contribution as part of the final product and receive recognition for that contribution. Successful property managers can involve their staffs in this type of challenge in any number of ways.

Due to their position the property manager has the most influence in setting the tone for a property staff. A fun atmosphere cannot be mandated but you can lead by example. If the manager sets a tone that involves challenging themselves to use creative and imaginative ideas to solve problems, his or her staff will do the same. If they strive to find joy and passion in every job they do it will inspire their co-workers.

However, if the manager develops a business as usual, don't bring me any new ideas I'm bored approach; the staff will generally also follow that lead.

Every job on a property has its own unique challenges and rewards. A manager that allows his or her staff to enjoy good-natured fun and encourages laughter can help everyone's day become more joyful, fun and productive.

Someone who is happy will be much more inclined to take pride in his or her work. Making sure that we take pride in our work is also another way to make a job more fun.

No matter how boring and repetitive a job is if approached with a positive attitude it can be accomplished with pride and satisfaction.

Best of all, the entire fun attitude is contagious. Not only for other workers but also for our customers. When a staff is having fun working it shows. Given a choice customers like to do business with people who are positive and having fun.

Team Fun

One property that I managed had problems with a vandal. Someone kept marking up the inside door of one of the elevators nearly every day.

The staff on that property had an immense amount of pride in the work that they were doing and how the property looked. Whoever the first staff person was that noticed any graffiti called it into the office. Within minutes one of the maintenance techs would be there with a can of paint and a brush to cover the marks.

The task was annoying because it didn't need to be done. Yet the staff took great pride in doing it because they were keeping the property neat and clean for themselves and their residents. They enjoyed their work even with the minor problems that were a constant part of their day.

It didn't take much time till the residents noticed what was going on and started to give positive feedback to the staff. The whole 80\20 rule again. The majority of the residents appreciated the pride that the staff took in the property and let them know. It was only a very small minority that was defacing the property and the staff worked hard to contain their efforts to ruin the property and enjoyment of their work.

Every manager should always be looking for ways to bring pride and fun into the workplace. The two are tied together. Taking pride in the work that you do will almost always translate into making the work fun. After all, you are going to be spending a large amount of your life at work, why not enjoy a little fun along the way.

This also goes right back to the concept of building a team. People who work together at a challenging job where they feel pride will bond and create a team much more capable than the parts that make it up. If a team is organized with an attitude of trust and fair treatment the bonds of history and shared experiences will create an atmosphere where laughter, playfulness and respectful teasing can thrive.

The most successful teams will be a mixture of diverse talents and views. A cohesive team will encourage and respect new ideas from all its members. The teamwork that grows into bonds and allows these diverse people to work together is amazing to watch. It will also create a fun atmosphere that will make work a whole lot easier, fun and productive.

While a single person can make their own job more interesting and challenging the concept has even more of an impact when a whole team is involved and motivated.

When the people on a team all start to approach their job in a more positive way the team will find ways to work together in unexpected ways. They will support each other and help each other complete their job. It becomes easier to maintain a positive attitude that presents itself as pride and sense of accomplishment.

A huge benefit will be the sense of responsibility that will come to a cohesive team. Instead of everybody only doing exactly what is in their job description and no more a team will support each other. They will support and help each other because they want to and not because they are ordered to help.

Creating a team that is willing to assist each other where needed will create a supportive atmosphere where your staff will be able continue to grow and be positively challenged. Everybody has up and down days. Yet when you work with people that you like and enjoy being around it will make everybody's job easier and smooth out the rough spots.

An important thing to remember is that what has worked in the past will not necessarily work in the future. In order to succeed both the property manager and the property staff must remain flexible and ready to adapt to changes as they happen. Bringing fun into the workplace will allow this while keeping everyone happier and less stressed.

One of the huge payoffs for running a happy staff will be that you will find it easier than ever before to recruit new staff members. Many times you'll discover that you have someone referred to you as soon as there is an opening. The best part is that your staff will only refer people to you that they think will be able to become part of your team. They don't want anybody that will gum up the works either.

Having a staff that can play while they work will allow them the opportunity to grow and excel. The ancient philosopher Socrates tried to teach that all things that are truly good flow from having achieved human excellence. Why not aim at true excellence in your staff by promoting fun at work.

There are many ways that you can encourage this attitude of fun at your property. First make sure that you as a manager checks any bad attitude at the door. Remember that you can't make people have fun but you can create an atmosphere where it can happen.

A manager who is light hearted and keeps the little daily disasters in perspective to the big picture encourages his or her staff to do the same thing. Being willing to laugh at yourself every once in a while is a great way to show that yes this is important but we will all make mistakes once in a while.

Always celebrate when your staff meets or exceeds major goals. Many times these goals have taken weeks or months to accomplish and that should be noted with a sigh of relief. Make sure that any success is a group success and you all share in it. To make a job fun and to create a sense of pride in their work, everybody needs to see how they helped accomplish the work that combined to reach each goal.

On a big project it is sometimes easy to get distracted from the big picture. Problems and decisions will be flying in on an hourly basis. Between the big and small problems the signs along the way that show your progress can be passed and forgotten.

It is important to make sure that does not happen. By showing your staff they are making clear progress you are showing them something they can take pride in. Sure they may be behind today with contractors or the corporate staff pushing to get this or that done. But for this few minutes they need to see that they set a goal and hit it. They got the job done. Just because the goal is a constantly changing target is no reason not to celebrate. As manager it is your job to motivate and show your staff how to have a little fun.

These celebrations can be small or big depending upon the size of the goal accomplished. A pizza for lunch where everybody gets a verbal and literal pat on the back can change a bad day into one where you can see some smiles.

Ask the families of your staff to as many of the functions as you can. A weekend BBQ or potluck is a great way for people to get together in an atmosphere other than work to socialize with co-workers and their families.

One property I know has a gag trophy that gets passed around. Any time somebody does a really bonehead mistake their name gets put on it and it sits on the shelf in the coffee room until someone else makes another silly mistake. A lot of lighthearted teasing goes along with the trophy and the manager makes sure it gets passed around a lot. It is always useful in getting some good-hearted laughs at a time when you might need them.

It is important to keep an eye on the stress level of your staff at all times. If someone is especially quiet or cranky talk to them and let them know that you care.

In a huge dysfunctional way a work team is like a family and everybody needs to look out for everybody else. As head of the house the manager will be able to help things along.

One task that should be in the job description of every on-site manager is keeping corporate staff off the backs of his or her staff so they can get their jobs done. This is obviously a slight exaggeration but not one that is too far from the truth.

Keep your supervisors away from your staff any time they are doing anything but being complimentary. It is hard enough for your staff to get a job done without having numerous people that are telling them you're not doing it right.

Have fun and celebrate when a staff member gets a promotion. The only good reason for a staff member to leave is if they get a promotion. A big part of your job should be to continually train and help your employees grow and improve. Find out what they want and in any way you can help them achieve their goals.

Not only will it help your employees advance, it will make your job much easier because people will want to work for you.

Occasionally give out a small treat to an employee just because they need the extra pat on the back. Let them off early or allow them to come in late.

Also remember that you don't need to have a success to celebrate. Sometimes having a party just because you are still there is enough to shake off a load of stress and get everybody back on track.

Creating a fun atmosphere at work will definitely help your bottom line. Everybody likes to deal with someone who has a genuine smile on his or her face. People will be more comfortable with your staff if they are more relaxed and approachable.

Listen to your employees and their needs. Knowing what is important to your staff will allow you to find opportunities to motivate your staff.

Always be ready to laugh at yourself. Be willing to be the butt of a joke when you deserve it. Nobody is perfect. Don't be the type of person who can dish out but can't take it. Not only will laughing keep you sane but it will also create a connection between you and your staff. This will make you much more accessible to your staff.

The staff that can play together will work better together. Remember that attitudes are contagious. You have to ask yourself if yours is worth catching.

"I have a simple but strong belief. The most meaningful way to differentiate your company from your competition is to do an outstanding job with information."

--Bill Gates--

Chapter Eight
Know What They Think

"They won't tell if you don't ask."

It has been said that you can't manage what you don't measure. In other words you can't change or improve how you interact with customers if you don't know what they are thinking about your service.

Surveys are one of the ways to get that information. They can answer a huge number of questions for you.

What do your residents think about you? Are you offering service that is better or worse than your competitors? Do they think that you are knowledgeable and responsive?

What is it that they like about you? In what areas do they think that you need improvement? Do your prospects think that you are offering anything special or are you just another face in the crowd?

What about your employees? Are they happy with the wages and benefits that you are offering? Do they understand or want a bonus system? How happy are they with your company?

Surveying your customers and employees can yield a goldmine in information. It's just that you need to ask them. As an industry we spend very little time researching the attitudes and desires of our customers. We rarely ask them what they like or don't like about our properties. Probably because we suspect that we are doing a much worse job than we think and don't want to hear about it.

In today's business climate we can't afford to loose valuable clients or staff. Surveys are a way to get the information we need to stay ahead of our competitors and satisfy the people we do business with.

Surveys are the second most commonly used management tool suggested by management gurus. The first is the mission statement. Yet the survey is generally the tool that has the highest financial rewards for companies that consistently and intelligently use it.

In the past we have operated apartment communities based on what we thought would make the residents happy. We would only change our methods when we were faced with slow renting vacancies. This is starting to change in a big way.

The information age is upon us. Those that collect and use their information to design their strategies proactively will be the biggest winners.

A part of this is that there is a growing distrust in what people say. This is especially true if that person is selling something.

Don't waste your time promising lofty goals or mission statements to your customers or your employees. Instead use concrete results to prove that you mean what you say.

Whether this distrust is true or not, an attitude that seems universal in our business is that we really know what the customer needs. Listen at your next managers meeting and you will likely hear all sorts of decisions being made on what our perceptions of what the customer wants. Time after time you see changes on properties with zero research on what our customers actual want or use.

In order to successfully compete in our changing market we as an industry have to get better at finding out what it is that our customers want. We need to research our client base to discover what it is that our customers really want. Then we need to use this information to develop services to satisfy them.

Our customers in the future are going to become more proactive in their desires and demands. They are going to be able to access more and better information about where they want to live. The communities that try to accommodate these desires are the ones that will find the most success.

An easy way to see how our industry uses information is to look at how most apartment communities are using web sites. Most web sites are basically an advertisement for how great the company is. Few even include a rudimentary resident survey even though this would be a perfect place for them.

A better use of a web site would be to create a satisfaction survey that can be filled out and the results seen in real time. Instant feedback that is so intensely in your face would have an enormously powerful effect if it was also shared with the people that deal with your customers.

Customers that use e-mail will also tend to include a more complete explanation of their problem than they would in a voice messaging system.

Think about how much easier your job would be if you knew exactly what it was that drew prospects to your property. What if you knew all the reasons that someone left your office without leasing? Could that change how you marketed your property?

Not only that but what about your current customers? If there was an avenue that they could use to quickly and easily notify you of problems would that make it easier to guarantee customer satisfaction which would translate very quickly into customer retention.

The key to have that happen though is to make sure that problems that are discovered in surveys are quickly addressed. The sooner that this happens the less possible damage will happen

A well-run property needs to know what is working and what needs to work better. Every prospect that comes into your office should leave with a postage paid pre-addressed card asking why they are going to lease or why they aren't. You could even set up a little computer kiosk in a corner where you ask prospects to answer a survey for some small gift to make it worth their time.

What was it that they liked and what didn't they like. Similarly, every prospect that ultimately moves in should be asked what made them decide to live at your property. What impressed them? What did you do right and what did you do wrong?

Residents should be periodically asked to respond to a questionnaire about how happy they are and what they would like to see done on the property.

Every time we get a complaint we should deliver a card to the resident to see how well we responded. Every time a work order is done a card should be left asking if the resident is satisfied.

A huge amount is budgeted towards advertising without anything spent on surveying our customer attitudes.

It should be easy for your customers and prospective customers to communicate with you. Whether it is by phone, fax, email, survey cards or questionnaires they should have multiple options for giving their opinion.

A lot of residents put their rent into envelopes to be dropped off at the office. Why not print up a bunch of envelopes with a simple survey on them and deliver them to your residents just before rent is due.

How To Survey

There are some pretty easy things to remember when you are asking people to complete a survey.

First you need to explain to whomever you are asking to do the survey why you need to have them complete it. Tell them how it is going to benefit them.

Make sure and keep the surveys simple and easy to complete. Long surveys will guarantee a lower response rate.

Think carefully about what it is that you would like to know. You can always tweak a survey to get answers to different questions but you generally won't be able to go back to the same people. Try to focus on specific questions where the results will actually be usable. Questions that are too general will not give you the information that you need.

Then you need to make sure to put some thought into how you are going to organize and use the information once you start to get responses. Decide what the questions are that you need to have answered. Decide who is going to handle the responses and how they are going to be tabulated.

Keep flexible when you start to see the returns. Don't print up too many of the postage cards or forms. You'll want to be able to modify the questions fairly frequently. Often the results of a survey will open new questions that you will want answered.

Many professionals suggest that you even use a third party to both collect and evaluate the information. They suggest this so that answers will be more truthful from the respondent and to avoid preconceived biases tainting the answers.

While this is a valid concern there are ways to handle them. Use postage paid postcards to a post office box so they won't be coming back to the individual properties. This will also allow a number of properties to use the same address. You can use some type of code on the card or address to differentiate the properties.

Questions should be carefully structured to avoid any misunderstandings. When you have a list of potential questions ask friends, family or customers if they interpret them the same way that you would. Different people will understand questions from different angles but a well thought out series of question will yield large amounts of information.

While it would be harder you can procure even more valuable information if you can schedule more in depth one on one interviews either in person or over a phone.

You can offer some type of reward or fee to entice people to take the time for these interviews. In a one on one interview you can explore answers to make sure that you understand them totally.

Start by asking yourself what it is that you would want to know. What would help you have an advantage over your competitors or better understand how to keep your clients happy?

Multiple-choice answers will allow answers to be more easily compiled and compared. Offer two positive and two negative answers. Use answers that will evoke an emotional response.

Instead of satisfactory, very satisfactory, unsatisfactory or very unsatisfactory use answers with emotional components. Try answers like fantastic, okay, pretty bad or lousy.

Then give them a fifth answer in case the question itself didn't apply. For instance use does not apply or not applicable.

Always give a space where the people being surveyed can write in a comment or observation. Simply ask if they have any other comment to make followed by a few blank lines. This will work even on a postcard. Longer surveys can include several questions that are open ended.

Employee Surveys

There is also a lot of value in doing surveys of your staffs. Especially in larger companies the lines of communication can get stretched a little thin. Few properties have a large enough staff to justify a survey but management companies should be looking at their employees all the time.

In a hierarchical organization employees are considered the cogs in a gear and to a large part expendable. Prior chapters have covered the ludicrousness of this viewpoint.

To succeed in the future economy the turnover that we accept today is going to have to be stemmed and controlled. One way to do this is to find out what the employee concerns are. Often time's problems are the result of misinformation or lacking information.

Employee surveys can help you focus on the needs and desires of your staff.

You need to encourage corporate staff to use this tool to get frank honest feedback from employees that will yield information that you can use at the property level.

Now Use The Research

This research is no good if no one uses it. Make sure that you keep an updated report of the responses that you receive. Keep the data in some sort of database so you can compare it over time and see if there are any trends of which you should be aware.

Don't expect that every survey you hand out will be returned. The number of responses will vary widely depending upon a large number of factors. The easier you make it for the people you are surveying to answer the more responses you will get.

Think outside the box to come up with new interesting ways for your customers to tell you what they think. The easier it is for them the more replies you will receive.

The more that you find out the more you will know what to ask. Questions will need to be clarified and changed to suit the market and which phase you are currently most interested in.

Make sure that the information is shared with all the people that are being rated in the survey. It is extremely frustrating to any staff member to know that surveys are being sent out to question how well they are doing their job when they don't find out the results.

You could place ongoing results on a bulletin board so your staff can see the results. Just make sure to keep the results current or change them at specific times. You will be amazed how interested the staff will be in how their work is being perceived. It can even be used as a tool to motivate a staff for better results.

Some sort of rewards program might be created to acknowledge meeting or exceeding satisfaction goals. Whether it is simply a pat on the back that gets tied into annual performance evaluations or an actual bonus would depend on your companies' corporate policies on performance bonuses.

There should also be rational thought out goals when it comes to using these survey results. Once surveys are consistently carried out they can be used as a monitoring system to observe results of new policies or advertising. Surveys can also be used to see what our customers or employees think of possible new policies.

For example, we may decide that our residents need to have a tennis court. But in a community of several hundred units, if only a few people want it, how good of use is the money we spent on it? Maybe the residents will point out that they would feel safer with more security lights. Without asking you won't get this information.

Don't limit your surveys to just one area. Even when certain surveyed areas seem to be satisfied, continue to periodically check back on them. Customer satisfaction is a changing target. Changes in the overall rental or employment market or any number of other possible influences can change the customers' perception of your property.

The ultimate importance and worth of surveys like these described are determined by how high in an organization they are consistently reviewed.

Bottom line is that there are two sets of information that need to be watched to maintain corporate success. They are the financials and the customer and employee satisfaction surveys. Failure to watch one will affect the other. Surveys can be used as an important tool to track how well we are responding to the current needs of our customers and to give insight into new needs.

The customer never forgets when they have a problem. Any problem that they have will color and influence your relationship with them for your entire relationship. When they are wisely used surveys can pinpoint problems while you can still do something about them.

Finally, simply receiving high marks in survey results should not be the goal. The key to any survey is to keep redesigning your survey to allow for continued improvements. If you are getting continual high marks you just might be asking the wrong questions. No one is perfect and there are sure to be problems lurking somewhere.

"Most battles are won before they are fought"

-- Sun Tzu--

Chapter Nine
Use Technology

"Make your life and job easier and less stressful."

Technology can be a wonderful thing. It can leverage your skills and allow you to accomplish much more in the same amount of time. The effective use of technology is a strong strategic weapon.

The Information Age has been with us for about 30 years. Yet most businesses continue to transact business in paper form. In our industry for the most part technology on properties is limited to financial reporting.

Fully using technology to your advantage can put you a large step ahead of your competitors. It can make your life easier and less stressful. Just by streamlining your paperwork you can save huge amounts of time that can be used elsewhere.

It is estimated that as much as 20-30% of an average office workers time is spent just looking for things. You can use day timers and computers to make sure that you are using technology as a tool to help organize and simplify your work.

The way the term technology is used here is anything that will help leverage your work. This means cell phones, computers, pda's, computer programs, e-mail and a myriad of other tools.

Nearly every office these days has a computer. Most have a fax. Many use e-mail. Yet few get the largest bang for the buck when using these tools. To this day many office staffs are still computer illiterate. The story that still makes the rounds is about the leasing person who thought the CD tray on her computer was a coffee cup holder.

A first simple example would be work orders. If they are being produced by hand you are wasting huge amount of time. There are a number of current programs designed to help automate your management office. Work orders should be put into some type of program that will sort them by unit, date and type. This will allow you to track and anticipate trends. The program you use should be able to print out a daily list of unfinished work orders so you and your maintenance supervisor can plan the work of the day.

How are the rental applications approved on your property? Does the property staff spend hours on the phone doing the work or are applications sent to a company that specializes in that type of work.

Credit check companies that specialize in apartment applications often use a scoring method to check applicants for fraud evictions, late payments and even criminal records. They can then issue a recommendation based on the criteria set by each property to approve or deny the application. The final decision is based on this recommendation and moves the manager into safer fair housing ground. All prospects are judged by the same criteria so claims of favoritism could not happen.

Think outside the box and go beyond that though. For instance, how often do you have to shut off the water in a building to make repairs? How many times have you or one of your staff had to walk the property delivering fliers telling your residents their water would be shut off the next day. Isn't this a huge waste of your time? How often does someone call right after you shut off the water for an emergency repair to complain they had just gotten in the shower or started a load of laundry.

Did you know there are simple inexpensive programs out there for your computer that can call selected numbers with a pre-recorded message? You could then quickly and easily identify which of your residents need to know and broadcast when repairs are going to happen with a few easy keystrokes. This can also be used to notify of other repairs to parking lots or roof repairs. You can notify if sections of the parking areas need to be kept clear for vendor parking or repairs.

It can even be used to deliver reminders on the rent due date to the residents that have not yet paid. You could remind them to include the late fee if it is late.

Many vendors are setting up web sites where you can place orders. Most of these can be customized to require PO numbers or approval of a specific person. This saves your maintenance supervisor immense amounts of time if they can use the computer to access and compare prices and delivery times. When the order is ready they can print out a legible list to get a purchase order for final approval before placing the order.

The phone itself is a marvelous tool. Yet generally we use it just for basics. Every one who answers the phone needs to confirm each residents phone numbers each time they call. Get their home, work and cell numbers. You need to make sure that each resident has a current number in your information database.

As an aside, many offices have more than one computer. Make sure they are networked so all information on all computers is the same and can be shared. Nothing will cause more frustration than not having your info up to date or having it on the wrong computer when you need it. Today it is relatively inexpensive to network computers to each other. You can even set up a wireless network in the office to allow the computers to communicate with each other and the Internet.

At least the manager and the maintenance supervisor should also have a property supplied cell phone. Better yet would be to have each staff member have one. Having supervisors that are easy to contact will solve all sorts of problems. Many problems are small if you deal with them quickly. It is only if they have time to grow that they get out of hand.

You can even get reasonably priced phones now that are a combination of cell phone and PDA. Once you have a PDA (Personal Digital Assistant) you'll wonder how you got along without it.

The PDA is a sort of electronic workbook. It will store copies of your schedule, appointments, to do list and phone numbers. You can use it to send and receive e-mail. The best part is it backs up to your computer so if you loose the PDA you'll still have all those phone numbers and names.

There are even programs written especially for these PDA's for any number of tasks. You can track your business expenses and the mileage on your vehicle. There are programs that will download maps for any area of the country along with lists of local restaurants, hotels and tourist spots. There are dictionaries and thesauruses and even full size books that you can load. Don't tell the boss but there are even really great games you can get on them too.

The PDA puts all this information at your fingertips in one place. To back it up and update the information to your computer you put the PDA in its cradle and punch a button.

The software that this information is stored in is called a personal information manager. It can be used by one or multiple persons to keep track of tasks and to do items. Once you start using a PIM to track phone numbers and your to-do items you will never go back to those hand written lists.

How often does a manager get after hour calls from the on call maintenance person about some problem on property? Wouldn't it be handy the next time that you get one of those calls to have easy access to every employee, vendor and resident phone number right in the palm of your hand

With the new phone/PDA's you can dial directly from your to do list or the phone directory. If a call comes in the caller ID will tell you the number and if it is in your phone directory the name and address information for that person will come up on your screen.

Current cell phones can also be bought with digital cameras and send and receive small pictures. Remember the saying that a picture is worth a thousand words. How often when you do a move out disposition have you had a unit that was trashed or had some specific damage?

Having pictures of the damaged unit will make your argument in case you have to go before a judge. Having them digital from your phone camera or even better a digital camera will make them easy to store and organize. A phone camera will make it easy to send a quick picture to either a supervisor or vendor to show them a problem or idea. The photos can be sent phone to phone or phone to e-mail. You can even get regular camera photos made into digital files for sharing or presentations.

Speaking of phones how many of you use a headset on your office phone. It's really a bad thing to do to your neck when you wedge the phone handset between your head and shoulder. A headset will keep your hands free and make it easier to handle phone calls while you shuffle papers. If you use a cell phone get one for your car too! It will make you a much safer driver. Best of all you won't get that painful crick in your neck.

Another easy way to save time is to automate as much paperwork as possible. Any document that is produced on a word processor can be linked to a database. Documents such as leases, lease renewal notices, 3-days and financial reports can be produced more quickly this way. You can personalize and track them. The best part is they will print out looking professional and be totally legible.

You can use multiple databases to crunch numbers and create financial statements for operating summaries. You can also use the databases to merge letter or documents for one to thousands of people. It is a quick and easy way to send a personalized letter to each of your residents.

If you are using a pen to fill in any report or document you are probably wasting time. You can easily take inexpensive courses from local schools or companies to learn how to convert forms into usable computer generated files.

If your management company doesn't have a web site for your community it's time for them to get one. They are relatively inexpensive given the huge benefits.

Surf the Internet and search for apartment communities to get ideas on what you can do. You'll find everything from simple to complex. Many are just a couple simple pages with contact information. Others offer a complete information pack. The best have sections for both residents and prospects.

A secure part of the site can even be set up for your employees to use. Easy access to information is going to be the phrase of the decade. How much time is spent every payroll producing the paperwork needed to generate the final reports. Each property does its own work and then send it to corporate where they put the information in other reports to generate the final paychecks.

Using secure access a corporate site could be set up to make it easy for property staff to sign in and out each day. All information could be accessible in whatever form the payroll department needed it without generated useless time consuming paperwork. Human resources could have all their forms available and easily streamline the payroll process and all associated paperwork. Job openings and new policy announcements could be posted.

Many web sites seem content to be an advertising medium for their community. A smart manager can get much more use out of them.

At the very least an apartment site needs to have numerous pictures of your community and apartments, a map to your location, floor plans, area information, rental rates, forms for work order requests, employee kudos forms, community policy rules, and information on your staff. Survey forms for residents and prospects could be included.

You can easily offer an up to date list of what types of units you have currently available. If your management company has multiple properties you should even be able to share this information between each property. It costs you a lot of money to get the prospects in your door. If you don't have the desired unit a little initiative on your part could get them to stop at a sister property.

It is typical of a hierarchal type of company to want to control access to vacancy information. It is usually a closely guarded secret to which few have access. An up to date vacancy list can put more information in the hands of the people that need it.

If you are running an efficient property with few vacancies a prospect seeing that will feel a sense of urgency. In any case having the vacancies showing which currently have applications on them will help sister properties know when they can refer to you.

It is easy to offer hyper links to other sites of interest. You could include links from your site to your corporate site, map sites, on-line newspapers, television stations, and various city directories.

We are becoming an around-the-clock society. There are more than 24 million Americans who work nightshifts. Our customers are expecting to be able to do business with us any time they want. You could think about expanding your hours or you could use technology to create easier access. Your residents should always be able to talk to maintenance 24 hours a day in case of an emergency. Using the Internet to allow them to access your office at the times they need you will be a substantial benefit to this group.

There is also the benefit of e-mail. E-mail is the most widely used application of the Internet. Allowing your residents to e-mail you will save huge amounts of time on the phone or writing actual hard copy letters. When a customer is unhappy the faster you respond the faster you can start to repair a frayed relationship. E-mail can help you do this.

The Internet is going to be used by more and more people as a tool of convenience. They are going to expect to be able to take virtual tours and complete applications on line. I've only seen a few sites where the resident can make an on-line payment or accept credit cards. In 2003 more than 34 million people handled their checking accounts on-line. This makes a decision a no brainer. Don't you want to make it as easy as possible for your residents to give you money?

You could even include a PDF file for a rental application that could be filled out and delivered directly to an on-line credit and risk evaluation service. This company could check the applicant and both of you would know that they are pre-qualified before they even come into your office. Much of the risk that is associated with fair housing violations during the leasing process could be completely sidestepped this way.

Most companies use technology as a management tool to increase the control that they have over finances. Think outside of the box and you will see there are many ways that you can use it to make your job easier. You can use it to market, contact residents, work resident retention, find and train employees and handle normal mundane paperwork that clogs your desk and time.

*"Only those who dare to fail greatly
can ever achieve greatly."*

-- Senator Robert Kennedy--

Chapter Ten
Trends to Keep an Eye On

"You get to where you're going, whether you plan the destination or not."

Predicting trends is the process of looking at the past through the lens of today and trying to focus on the future. It is attempting to see where trends will emerge and where they might go. Trends are defined as long-term changes that affect large populations across a wide variety of industries.

In our current weak economy many property management companies are under intense pressure to perform better financially.

Day in and day out this often forces the apartment manager into operating in a crisis mode. Even in the best of times most companies are lucky to complete next years budget. Planning for trends that will take years to mature takes a special type of foresight and perseverance.

Yet it is precisely those companies that plan ahead and see opportunities in future trends that always enjoy the greatest success. Business as we know it is in the process of changing forever. Information technology advances will affect the way that we do everything. With that in mind let's polish up the old crystal ball and see what we can envision.

Trends already in play will continue to foster change in our industry even faster in the future than they have in the past. These changes will affect the most basic ways that our industry conducts business.

Part of the response to emerging trends will be an increase in market niche specializations as we seek to keep buildings full and look for new opportunities.

In 1960 an estimated 38% of the population moved at least every 15 months. Today that number has grown to more than 51%. Advances in communications and technology will continue to make us an increasingly mobile society.

While in many ways the Internet is not causing the changes it does help enable them. The Internet just turbo charges the changes that are already happening. To a large extent it is the advances in information technology that are making many of these changes possible.

The majority of problems in business can be traced to information problems. When people have incorrect or incomplete information they often make bad decisions that are based on faulty perceptions.

What information technology does is not just make more information available faster. More importantly it organizes the information to make it more usable. Where reports and financial information used to be months behind what was actually happening it now could be instantly available.

Retail juggernaut Wal-Mart has one of the most advanced reporting systems in business. They can tell you instantly how many of what items were sold each day. By using technology to deal more closely with their vendors and monitor their inventory on a day-by-day basis they can minimize costs while maximizing profits. It is no coincidence that they have grown into the largest corporation in the world.

The way that many people are employed is also evolving. In the past careers were linear and had definite goals and advancement opportunities. A growing current trend is for employers to hire people as contractors on a project-to-project basis. This allows the employer to have control of the project while still limiting long-term employee obligations.

Instead of doing the same tasks for years these people will work on specific projects until completion. Many will transfer from company to company, as their skills are required for a specific period of time. While this will make a persons income less certain it will make a work career more interesting and challenging. The people with the most flexible skills will be most in demand and will move where the work is.

Current low interest rates have increased home ownership by more than 4% since 1995 bringing it to the highest levels in forty years. At the same time many apartment residents are moving into their prime home buying years and will move out of our apartments. A smaller group of echo boomers are taking their place. This is happening at a time when it is actually cheaper to own than rent.

As a society we've also developed a taste for good living. The average size home has increased from 1,140 square feet to more than 2,225 square feet, according to Harvard University's Joint Center for Housing Studies.

It has been predicted that many of the people who live in these larger homes will eventually enter back into the rental market as they downsize after their families grow up and move out. Numerous companies are currently upgrading the apartment unit sizes that they operate based on this forecast.

It is also expected that the retiring baby boomers will demand both larger and more luxurious apartments. In addition, as their children the echo boomers move out on their own before they buy homes they are going to want to live in apartments that remind them of their parents' larger homes.

Yet there is another trend that was illustrated in a recent report that the AARP did on its 35 million members over the age of 50. It stated that 45% of its members planned on working to at least 70 or beyond. It's not just because they are more physically fit than their parents. Many of the people in this group are heading towards retirement age while less financially prepared to retire than their parents.

Millions of these people have seen their retirement savings devastated by the recent stock market collapse. Even as markets recover these boomers are becoming more conservative. Meanwhile, the parents of the boomers are also living longer and running up large medical bills. Five out of six boomers expect no inheritance from their parents to aid in their own retirement.

The cost of health insurance, long term care and prescriptions are all soaring. The younger boomers are also reporting that the current trend toward shifting the risks of retirement savings to the individual is making them increasingly nervous about the thought of retiring.

At the same time many other people are not adequately prepared for retirement. Another study by Employee Benefits Research Institute reveals that 61% of workers have never even calculated their retirement needs.

These facts contradict the excepted theory that the boomer generation will retire and leave the job market in masse. The truth is that many of this generation may not be able to afford it.

That is good news for the thousands of older properties that have smaller size units. There will continue to be a good market for well run economically priced units.

Yet there can be little doubt that the future for most apartment market areas contains a major shift in power. The apartment owners and managers are facing a better educated more demanding market than ever before.

The Internet today is but a shadow of the Internet of tomorrow. The huge amounts of information that will be easily available in the future will put the residents in the drivers seat but a shrewd manager can make sure they are along for the drive.

Virtual tours, area information, satisfaction ratings, crime statistics and information on every apartment available will become so easy to access that prospective residents will become more savvy and knowledgeable about rental properties than was ever possible in the past.

By the time that these prospects finally come to your property they will know everything about you and your competitors. They will know unit sizes, layouts and prices. They will know what is available and who is offering specials.

To benefit from these trends and stand out among the competition apartment managers will use innovative in-unit and on property amenities to increase the level of service that can be provided to their residents. The number and variety of these services provided will increase dramatically along with the flexibility in their use. Information technologies will be the source of many of these new opportunities for growth as we discover new ways to use them.

Flexibility in the apartment industry will ultimately mean giving our residents more options. Creating affordable term housing through mass construction of cookie cutter apartments has dominated property design in the past. All the units were planned and built the same to keep costs down.

Our future in the digital age is going to change that approach. People are going to want to customize their individual units to an extent never before possible.

The founder of Dell Computer, Michael Dell, coined the term "mass customization". He used that term to describe the changes he foresaw in the way consumer expectations were going to be affected by high tech advances. He felt that consumers would become more insistent on having quality products and services that fit their specialized needs.

Dell Computer has become a model for the way this can be accomplished. Instead of stores having mass-produced Dell computers on display, units are custom ordered on-line or by phone with only the unique options that the consumer desires and is willing to pay to receive.

As consumers are able to customize other purchases in their life it is inevitable that eventually it will affect our industry. This might ultimately include designing more flexible units that could be altered or changed using movable walls and upgradeable appliances.

Still, a first step to accomplish this would be to allow our residents to have more input into the decorating and color schemes of their units. Add-ons such as security alarm units and appliance upgrades can also easily become an added incentive common in most existing units.

Much like commercial leases, residents of the future will be able to choose to upgrade their units from the base available unit by amortizing the improvements over the life of their lease. These upgrades might include upscale appliances, personalized wall colors, custom room layouts, upgraded carpets or other options in floor and window coverings. Kitchens and bathrooms will be offered with upgrades such as custom cabinets and countertops. Upgraded fixtures will allow the resident to customize each unit to their specialized taste and needs.

Not only will this customization become a huge marketing advantage to the properties that use it, it will also strongly encourage the residents to stay for longer terms in their units and combat turnover.

The current smart card that is being used on some properties as a prepaid laundry card is another example of an emerging trend. Since 30% of service calls for laundry machines involve the coin slides using smart cards increase profits while decreasing problems for both the laundry company and property management

In Japan vending machines are being introduced that accept payment from cell phones. You simply punch in a code in the phone and it beams an authorization along with the information needed to deduct that amount from your bank account.

Veterinarians currently are inserting small chips into dogs and cats. When scanned these contain information about the pet, who its owner is and contact information. Recently this type of chip was implanted in a small test group of people to test the chip as an identification and financial tool.

It takes only a small leap of the imagination to see that these chips could easily simplify our lives. If people can get past the idea of big brother tracking us these could be a wonderful thing. Imagine being able to leave the house and never have to worry about carrying ID, cash, keys or credit cards. These chips could carry information not only for financial transactions but also things like medical records.

The same idea could be modified to work as an entry key. They could be used to access property business centers and identify the user to charge for computer or business machine usage. They might also be used to control access to pool and work out areas allowing these to become additional profit centers. Charges for all kinds of additional services could be simplified using these chips.

Lease terms and conditions will also become more negotiable. It is estimated that currently only 15% of our population will rent their entire lives. Other people will rent while they save to purchase their own home. However, a growing portion of the population of the future will become lifestyle renters. These are people who will demand more and better services.

As we continue to try to retain our residents' longer-term leases will become more desirable. Annual rent increases for longer term leases will still be possible by basing them upon some outside factor like the consumer price index.

More properties will become pet friendly and allow residents to amend the terms of their leases more easily to include or exclude roommates as they move in and out.

In addition to things like parking and pet fees that we already charge, flexible amenities might include more lifestyle options. A separate fee for use of property amenities like the pool, workout room, or business office might be charged on a per use or monthly basis. Marketing agreements with neighboring businesses like gyms or carwashes would increase the range of services a property could offer.

As the office becomes more automated tracking and billing these charges will become easier and increase profit potential. Residents could choose to have a monthly bill sent to them that they then could pay for electronically. Few properties currently accept credit cards or electronic payment. This will change as we strive to accommodate the desires and needs of our residents.

Information technology will also allow properties to become a central clearinghouse for other premium services. Our average renter is facing an increasingly busy life.

Aggressive apartment managers will take advantage of that trend. Premium services such as housecleaning, errand running, dog walking, grocery delivery and laundry services can be easily offered through subcontractors or business alliances.

This will make leases less likely to be at a set rate. Instead numerous options with various fees will allow the resident to tailor their rent to the lifestyle and options that they prefer.

Flexible amenities will encourage a continuance of the current trend of bill backs and the unbundling of services. A lot of larger communities have already separated heating, water and sewer charges from the base rent.

A possible negative will emerge when residents realize that by paying these fees they are taking all motivation away from the owner to upgrade and make heating and cooling systems more efficient and cost effective. However this can also be used as a marketing benefit.

Advertising these bill backs as a financing source to fund upgrading of energy efficient and water saving appliances and fixtures will place apartment communities in line with another strong future trend towards greener communities.

Our residents will demand better use of natural resources. Any property that emphasizes this will be a step ahead of their competition.

Specialized marketing campaigns to deal with the coming trends will need to be developed. These might include resident retention programs designed beyond retaining residents to a specific property or unit. To serve an increasingly mobile population it will become necessary to capitalize on the things that will appeal to them.

The definition of the term resident retention will change from retaining a resident in a specific property unit to maintaining business ties in different properties and unit types over their rental life,

Benefits such as transferable "seniority" that would include rent discounts and special decorating benefits would inspire a resident to keep renting from a specific management group. Close ties to referral services and moving services would allow a lasting relationship with residents to be formed and maintained.

Another part of this strategy would require landlords to enable residents to move more easily among units of various sizes and locations as their needs changed.

Advances in information technology will be one of the most powerful forces behind these changing needs. Having information available instantly will allow managers to respond to changes in the market faster. One interesting area of the near future is how the Internet will change how we market and run our properties.

In 1776 Adam Smith described free markets in *The Wealth of Nations.* His theory was that if every buyer knew every sellers price, and every seller knew what every buyer was willing to pay, everyone in the market would be making informed decisions and societies resources distributed more efficiently.

One interesting phenomenon right now is the auction sites that have sprung up. These sites take away the advantage of size and allow even small businesses to sell on a more even playing field. This approaches the ideal that Adam Smith was describing.

The Internet makes it easier than ever for prospective purchaser to compare products. More than 126 million Americans regularly use the Internet. Nearly a third of these have access to high-speed connections. As these connections become faster, easier and cheaper it is inevitable that the ripple effects will impact how apartment communities do business.

Prospective renters will expect more information to be easily available to them. They will also expect to be able to compare communities. It will become much easier to check area information like crime statistics, local parks, entertainment and convenience to the things they need every day.

Just for a moment imagine what this might be like when this happens. A resident in a community gets notice at work that they are going to be transferred to a new location. They decide that they are going to move to save on commuting time.

Sitting on the couch in the living area they think for a minute. Then they will verbally give the computer the following information. "Find me an apartment within a fifteen minute drive of my new job location. I want something with a wood burning fireplace and carport. A pool is nice but not super important. They must be within walking distance to a park, have a coffee shop on the way to work and have a Victorian feel to it. I'll want an east-facing unit with plenty of big windows and a private patio to barbeque on. It must have a workout room that includes a sauna."

While the resident is describing what he or she wants the computers intelligent agent program is already starting to scour the Internet databases for the answer.

The agent knows that its owner has a twenty-pound dog and will want a one bedroom with an office. With lightening speed it looks for all properties within a fifteen-minute drive of the new office then eliminates those that don't take dogs.

It eliminates those that don't have patios. It eliminates several more because they don't have wood burning fireplaces. Then contacting the properties it sorts through the parameters for the unit to see how many are currently available. Seeing that XYZ Management runs two of the units it automatically drops those. Its' owner had a bad experience with that company.

Almost as soon as its' owner is finished speaking a list of available units pops up on the screen. There are five available. None have a satisfaction ranking above 70%. "May I suggest that you accept a property with a workout gym on the way to your work?" The agent asks. Its' owner accepts the suggestion.

Now there are ten units available with the highest ranking of 82%.

"May I also suggest that you look at units that have gas fireplaces," the intelligent agent again suggests. Again its' owner accepts the suggestion.

The list now grows to 14 units with the highest ranking of 93%. "Show me the top three possibilities." The owner instructs. Side by side photos of each property instantly appear on the wall screen. Under the photo is the name of the property and its price. After a minute a different view is shown, then another. "Show a side by side comparison of the first and third property." The two properties are shown first with a site plan, then the specific unit available and its floor plan, a view of the patio, another of the covered parking and finally the fireplace.

"Show me the kitchens and baths." The wall screen again changes showing the layouts with changing photos below showing the appliances and fixtures.

"The first possibility is managed by the same company that runs your current complex. They indicate that they will allow an immediate transfer of your current lease with no penalty, pay the first $300 of a moving company fee or allow you to use that as a rent credit or decorating allowance."

"Good set me an appointment for them." The agent looks into its owner's day timer and contacts the intelligent agent at the apartment community. Comparing schedules they agree to set the appointment for next Tuesday.

While this may sound futuristic it is closer than you might think. Information technology will enable our typical resident to have easy access to massive amounts of information.

One of the interesting things that the on-line auction sites do is allow buyers to rate sellers and visa versa. It is not inconceivable that some of the rental sites or even some dedicated special site would start to carry satisfaction ratings received from residents. Residents might be contacted after they move in to answer questionnaires. They would be asked to rate each property based on how happy they were with a number of different criteria.

Word of mouth has always been a huge factor in the buying decision of the average renter. Some surveys estimate that people relying at least partly on word of mouth to decide where to rent run as high as 80%.

There are even a few companies that are testing offering apartments in hotter markets at auction right now. While it doesn't seem very conceivable that the typical property would allow its apartments to be offered in an auction it is that they will respond much quicker to market changes. Knowing exactly what is empty around you and what is going to be available will encourage a more flexible price. The set price written in stone that is the hallmark of our communities now will fall with barely a whimper.

A better use for auction sites would be in a slow market. If you have vacancies in your building that have been empty for a while it costs a lot of money. How tempted might you be to auction these empty apartments for the best price that you can to get them occupied?

Using digital technology to streamline new processes will radically improve how flexibly managers can respond. At heart most business problems are often information distribution problems. More efficient information distribution will allow managers the full benefit of all their employees' capabilities while giving them the speed to compete in the emerging high-speed business world.

The most successful property managers of the next decade will use digital tools to reinvent the way they work. Doing this will allow these managers to make quick decisions and use their resources most efficiently. It will allow them to service their customers faster in increasingly positive ways.

The very way that we manage our buildings will have to change. Apartment units will become more intelligent. Energy use, security, communication, rent collection and problem solving will all become more automated.

Imagine a thermostat that will contact the office and request a work order automatically if it senses that the correct temperature is not being maintained. Refrigerators and stoves of the future will send out warnings if they are about to malfunction. Sensors that detect and notify offices of water leaks will catch problems while still small. Maintenance can become more preventative and less crisis oriented.

Residents are also becoming more concerned with their personal security. Alarm systems and security monitoring will become a valuable amenity. Keyless entry systems that read fingerprints or require pass codes will become more popular. Security of units can be remotely monitored while their residents are at work or on vacation. Gated communities with controlled access will continue to gain in popularity.

For residents, information technology will offer a wide array of new services. There will be new entertainment options well beyond what is currently available.

At the same time it is estimated by some that the number of people telecommunicating will increase to nearly 75% of the population by 2010.

This increase in home workers will require a significant change in our current management processes. Their needs will require new unit designs with a dedicated workspace and the latest telecommunications capabilities.

People will become more involved in using telecommunications and information technology for entertainment and to educate their children and themselves.

These changes will be upon us rapidly. Hardest to predict is when one trend crosses another and sparks an unexpected outcome.

Who would have guessed ten years ago that so many apartment communities would see the value of having a web site? Or for that matter known what a web site was.

The information that is being posted on these sites was already there and available if you went into the leasing offices. What the Internet did was make it possible to see and use this information any where in the world with in seconds.

It made it possible for someone across the country to look at and choose an apartment in our communities. It made it easy to complete the application and lease paperwork in a few hours instead of weeks.

This is the brave new world that we are entering. This is the world we need to conquer to enjoy passionate lives full of joy and happiness.

__Conclusion__

The one constant in this universe is change. You can always be sure that things will change. The people that are the most likely to succeed are the ones that can adapt to those changes.

They will succeed because they prepare for the changes with education, experience and attitude.   They keep an open and flexible mind by being curious and willing to try new things.

Many people in our industry are stuck in the past. They do things because that is how they always have been done. Kicking and screaming they might get pulled into using computers but that will only automate what they have always done.

It's like the story of the new bride and her husband. Cooking their first dinner the bride took out the ham and prepared it just as she had learned from her mother.

Before she put the ham in the pan she cut the end off. Placing it in the pan she then put it into the oven to cook.

Curious the husband asked why she had cut the end of the ham off. His wife replied that was the way her mother had always done it. Later that week the husband asked the mother why she cut off the end of the ham before cooking it. She replied that was the way that her mother, his wife's grandmother had always done it.

The next time that the husband met the grandmother he asked her why she cut of the end of the ham before cooking. The grandmother replied that it was because her pan was to short for a full size ham so she had to cut the end off to make it fit.

The moral of the story is that procedures get started in odd ways. Usually to fill a need and sometimes because of a quirky owner or manager.

Doing something because that is the way that it has always been done is a sure recipe to mediocre performance.

Compare how our industry uses it's technology and people compared to many other businesses and you'll see one glaring fact.

Apartment communities tend to use technology to streamline accounting. Very little is used to make the employees jobs easier or to make them more efficient. In fact, because of extra demand for financial information and increased paper work due to legal concerns, the average manager is handling far more paper work than ever before.

In order to be the creative manager who succeeds in the future you need to continually examine and question why things are being done in a certain manner.

Always be watching other businesses to see what they are doing and what new innovations they are trying.

Bottom line is that property management is a service business. If you want to succeed you need to give better service than your competitors. Do this and it will also make your job much easier.

INDEX

Advertising   55

Apartment Association20

Apartment Models   64

Asbestos   9

Auction Sites   164

Big Picture   124

Business Climate   59

Buyers Market   59

Complaining   50

College Degrees   7

Corporate Staff   42

Curb Appeal   104,112

Dell Computer   156

Difficult People   37

E-Bay   60

Employee

    Bonuses   81

    Communication 85,86

    Compensation 81

    Criticism   87

    Dress   18

    Employment   12,153

    Empowerment76,79

    Evaluation   82

    Pay Structure 82

    Retention   88,90

    Rewards   124,125,126

    Self Evaluation16

    Skills   17,20

Surveys	130,135	
Training	61	
Fair Housing	9	
Fun	115,119,121	
Grocery Store	117	
Hierarchy	19,25,76,136,148	
Humor	118,124,126	
Inferior Work	80	
Information Age	130,152,161	
Internet	59,161	
Landscaping	104	
Lead Paint	9	
Leasing		
	Activities	69,97,100,108
	Agent	65
	Sizzle	101
	Buttons	101
	Options	157,158
	Phone	111
Legal Climate	8	
Manager	7,11,21,41,74	
Marketing	102,103,160	
Mass Customization	156	
Mission Statement	58,131	
Motivation	73,74,76,81,116	
Mystery Shoppers	99	
Newsletters	69,70,103	
Paperwork	43	
Passion	8,11,15,120	
Pride	120	
Project Proposals	30	

Property Info   59
Property Management11,77
Property Owners   7,8,22
Rent   45
     Late   46,143
     Raises   40
     Specials   107
Rental Applications   142
Resident
     Current   66,105,132
     Future   132
     Leaving   67
     New   64
     Past   56
     Problem   44,47,68
     Referral Fees   106
     Surveys   68,132
     Unhappy   91,92
Resident Retention   53,65,70
     Activities   53,66
     Budget   54
     Contacts   54,132
Retirement   155
Sister Properties
     Sharing Info   55
     Tours   55
Smart Card   157
Stress   10
Staff   24,61,73,77,78,93
Surveys   69,129,133,136,138
Team Work   25,61,121,122,123,125

Technology   141,159,164
Tools
    Cell Phones   145
    PIM   24,154
    PDA   144
Trends   113,151,166
Turnover   9,21,57
Unbundling Services   159
Vendor   29
    Approved   29
    Back up   33
    Pricing   32
Wal-Mart   153
Web Site(s)   103,131,145,147,155,166
Work Orders   92,143

BOOK ORDER FORM

==

   To order additional copies please send $19.50 per book for surface shipping. Shipping may take three to four weeks. Quicker delivery by air mail available for $3.50 per book.

Please send the following books:

____ copies of **Apartment Property Management= $**_____

Shipping   ($2.00 per book land/$3.50 Air)   = $_____

                                   Total Cost = $_____

Postal Orders can be mailed to:

   Pinnacle Apartment Services LLC

   PO Box 9719

   Denver CO 80209

Please send check or money order payable to Pinnacle Apartment Services. In order to order by credit card go to aptresults.com or your local bookstore.

Ship order to:

Name:_____

Address:_____

City:_____ State:_____ Zip:_____

_____ Check here if you would like to receive notice of more books from this author. You can also register at aptresults.com.

BOOK ORDER FORM

==

      To order additional copies please send $19.50 per book for surface shipping. Shipping may take three to four weeks. Quicker delivery by air mail available for $3.50 per book.

Please send the following books:

____ copies of **Apartment Property Management= $_____**

Shipping   ($2.00 per book land/$3.50 Air)   = $_____

              Total Cost = $_____

Postal Orders can be mailed to:

     Pinnacle Apartment Services LLC

     PO Box 9719

     Denver CO 80209

Please send check or money order payable to Pinnacle Apartment Services. In order to order by credit card go to aptresults.com or your local bookstore.

Ship order to:

Name:_____

Address:_____

City:_____ State:_____ Zip:_____

_____ Check here if you would like to receive notice of more books from this author. You can also register at aptresults.com.

Printed in the United States
31057LVS00005B/184-186